# MEMO
# MEMORIALS

*My Life in Monuments to the War Dead*

# Michael Aidin

SYNCLINE
PRESS

First published in the United Kingdom in 2017
by Syncline Press
The Old Rectory, Wiggonholt, Pulborough,
West Sussex RH20 2EL
email: office@michaelaidin.com

The illustration on the cover of this book features a fantasy of famous
war memorials in a Sussex landscape mural painted by local artist
Elizabeth Butler from the Aidins' dining room wall.

This book is a work of non-fiction based on the life, experiences
and recollections of the author. Every precaution has been taken
to verify the accuracy of the information contained herein and to
acknowledge the right of copyright holders. In the event of any
omissions or errors the author will be pleased to rectify these
matters in future editions of the work.

A CIP record of this book is available from the British Library.

ISBN 978-1-5272-1245-9

# ✎ Contents ✎

# ✧ Introduction ✧
# A World at War

*The Relief*

One of my earliest childhood memories is being shown from my pushchair the balcony of the Lion Hotel in Pembroke, South Wales, and being told that was where Lord Nelson appeared with Emma, Lady Hamilton. I had no idea who these people were except that they were clearly very important.

When I was a small boy I read that in the Napoleonic Wars, news was distributed throughout the country by mail coaches from London. If the news was good, the coaches were decorated with laurel, if the news was bad the coaches were draped with black crepe. After Trafalgar, the coaches were draped with crepe because the death of Nelson was regarded as a far greater loss than his stunning victory. At Lloyds, the Lutine Bell, traditionally rung twice for the return of a ship or once for the loss of a ship, was rung only once, such was the tragedy of the loss of Nelson.

Some time ago I met Sir John Kerr, First Sea Lord, who said that if Nelson had survived the battle, he would probably have spent the rest of his life making a nuisance of himself at the Admiralty and filling the Sunday papers with his goings on. When I lived in New York, I would tell my American friends they could make jokes about anyone in England, the Queen, Mrs Thatcher, but never jokes about Nelson.

Lord Nelson's most famous monument is the Column in Trafalgar Square which was erected about forty years after his death. Some years ago, on a bus going around the Square, I heard a tourist asking the conductor, 'Who is the guy on the pillar?' He replied, 'That's Admiral Nelson who, one hundred and ninety-seven years ago today, defeated the combined fleets of France and Spain at the Battle of Trafalgar.' No more questions from the tourist. I tell this story because it shows the significance of Nelson in British folk memory. However, I have a question about Nelson's Column. Is it a war memorial? Does it commemorate our greatest naval hero, killed in the moment of victory, or does it commemorate a naval victory which gave Britain a century of supremacy at sea?

In Napoleonic times, not much was known about the conditions of the war on the battlefield but with the advent of film, the reality of war and the death of millions of men in the Great War remains a heavy cloud over the collective memory of the British and the inhabitants of many other countries. Most families have unspoken faded memories of the war dead. One day at the war memorial at Arundel, West Sussex, I found a British Legion cross with a poppy pressed into the ground with the inscription: 'To the granddad we never knew.'

In 1914, my father was about to leave one of the leading Protestant schools in Ireland. He went to medical school and many of his school friends and companions joined up and were killed. Most men did not discuss their war experiences and my father likewise never said anything about his lost companions and to my regret I was never brave enough to ask him what he remembered of the Troubles, except he once said things went on surprisingly normally notwithstanding.

My mother's sister was a young school teacher at the time of the Great War and I think her memory was haunted by the young soldiers she knew who went to France to die.

My wife's grandfather was killed in the Great War, before seeing his baby daughter, my wife's mother. The family assumed that he was among the missing with no known graves. However, a report of his death was subsequently found amongst some family papers. Through the Commonwealth War Graves Commission, I traced his grave in Northern France. I took my in-laws, both over eighty, to see the grave where, in an emotional moment, flowers were placed. My wife could not face the trip. This was a stressful visit because my father-in-law was severely injured in Italy in the Second World War when my wife was a tiny baby. He was reported missing, presumed lost. Eventually he was found in a British Military Hospital in Naples with serious wounds.

Until over fifty years ago, war memorials were very much at the back of my mind. My job had involved a good deal of travel and in my work and after I retired, I saw memorials to the war dead in many countries of the world. During my travels, I marvelled at the scale of memorialisation to the war dead. Visiting France, I developed an interest in memorials to the Great War and the French Pacifist memorials. I saw several monuments in

Germany while arranging an aviation deal in divided Berlin. One negotiation in Düsseldorf broke down when Thomson's MD, an ex-RAF group captain, was asked if he'd ever been to Düsseldorf before. He replied, 'In Düsseldorf, no. Over Düsseldorf, twice.'

I am a great believer when travelling to a new country to find out about its culture and its people. Looking at memorials enables us to understand better the attitudes of people in that country. They are an insight into contemporary society, of artistic currents and the cross-fertilisation of cultural ideas, of racial and social integration or dissolution and of changing religious views. The study of war memorials consists of an understanding of the attitudes of the past and can facilitate the interpretation of history, and in a sense the public veneration of the war dead is in Carl von Clausewitz's famous phrase 'war is nothing but a continuation of politics by other means.'

Returning from a business trip to Germany, I travelled by train across the empty fields of Eastern France to Châlons-sur-Marne (now renamed Châlons-en-Champagne for the sake of the French wine industry) where I met my wife with one of our daughters. Outside the Cathedral, we saw a monument to the dead of the First World War showing a French officer leading his men laden down with equipment struggling through the mud of the Western Front. The title of the group was *'Le Relève'* (the Relief). The sculptor was Gaston Broquet (*1880-1947*), now largely forgotten but almost one hundred years ago, his war memorial work was popular with the French public, resonating with the feelings in the country which in the war lost one and a half million of its men, and nearly every family lost a member. This monument seemed to sum up the misery, horror and ultimate futility of the First World War.

From that time, I started to look seriously at war memorials. Normally, a war memorial is a monument, but it can be a speech, a piece of music, a church or other building, or even a scholarship endowment. War memorials can also take the form of poems, music or pictures. John Singer Sargent's murals at Harvard University commemorate the First World War dead. Poetry plays an important role. Some of Walt Whitman's finest poetry reflects emotions evoked by his work as a medical orderly in the Civil War. One of the most well-known memorial poems is Tennyson's 'The Charge of the Light Brigade' which for many years after the Crimean war was known to nearly every English-speaking school child and still resonates in the British National consciousness.

Benjamin Britten set the First World War poetry of Wilfred Owen to music in his War Requiem. The poem 'Casabianca' written in 1826, by English poet Felicia Hemans (1793-1835), commemorates an actual incident that occurred in 1798 during the Battle of the Nile aboard the French ship Orient.

An extract of the poem reads:
*'The boy stood on the burning deck,*
*Whence all but he had fled;*
*The flame that lit the battle's wreck*
*Shone round him o'er the dead.'*

There are other less polite versions which are in common use. This may not seem usual in modern war poetry but in her lifetime Felicia Hemans outsold Byron.

I became aware that memorials to the war dead were not only the most common form of public monument but occasionally were moving works of public art. The tragedy of war has produced many fine works of art as memorials to the fallen, which tell a story of courage and sacrifice. Many of the finest artists of the past two hundred years were caught up in the war enthusiasm of their generation including Picasso (Guernica), Maillol (Banyuls-sur-Mer memorial), Lutyens (Thiepval memorial), Augustus Saint-Gaudens (Robert Shaw memorial) and the illustrious American architectural firm of McKim, Mead and White and the distinguished artists who worked with them.

The earliest memorials were simple steles, a stone or wooden slab (there is no satisfactory equivalent word in English). Gradually in the nineteenth century, angels began to appear on graves in public cemeteries. The earliest military grave memorials were wood and were subsequently replaced with marble gravestones in the period after the US Civil War (1861-65). In later conflicts, European countries such as Germany, France and Italy have crosses on their military graves but curiously the British have not placed crosses on military graves. In America, Christian symbolism is unknown on public monuments to the war dead. In England, the war memorial, on a typical village green, consists of a cross with the names of the fallen from the local area inscribed on its base, usually starting with the First World War. This is an important difference between England and the United States.

War memorials also give an indication of national attitudes to war. For example, many war memorials in France to the Great War show mourning women, dying soldiers and a few are overtly pacifist, with the inscription 'Maudit la Guerre' (cursed be war). Anti-war memorials are virtually unknown in the English-speaking world. If the Americans and the British had studied these pacifist memorials in France, would they have been surprised by the fall of France in 1940? War memorials or their absence, may sometimes reveal more than history books about the emotional cost and impact of war upon the national psyche.

I was once asked what my emotions were when I see a war memorial. Some years ago, I was looking at the Battle of Britain Memorial on the Thames Embankment. Reading the names, I came across a Sgt Burt. His name stirred a memory. I remember being at school in the Chapel at the unveiling of the Second World War memorial. We sat by forms, boys seated in alphabetical order. The boy next to me was called Burt. I had always thought him reticent, self-contained, and inarticulate, but he was in tears. I pointed to the list of the fallen with the name Burt and asked if it was a relation. He said it was his brother. This certainly bought the tragedy of his loss home to me. I had forgotten about the incident until the name Burt on the memorial jogged my memory. I checked with the school and they were able to confirm that a Nigel Burt, my contemporary, had lost a brother in the Battle of Britain.

We all probably remember the old, old men, who were the last survivors of the First World War, who were unable, although obviously very brave, to restrain their tears at the Cenotaph, thinking of the horrors they had seen and the friends they had lost. As one becomes older one becomes more emotionally affected by these incidents.

A few years ago, I met a retired teacher from Lancashire at a seminar about casualties in war at the Wellcome Foundation in London. This old lady, who appeared to be in her eighties, was sitting alone. I asked why she had come. She said she was unhappy about the way some memorials to the war dead were maintained. Her fiancée had been killed in an air crash in Cumbria in the 1940s training Commonwealth pilots. A memorial had been erected after the war but the current vicar who was a pacifist didn't care for war memorials. She had written to the Canadian and Australian governments telling the story of the neglect. They sent their Air Attaches up from London with a representative of the RAF. Arrangements were made to restore the memorial. She must have been pretty tenacious. I wonder if the pacifist vicar knew what had hit him.

# ✧ Chapter One ✧
# A War Child

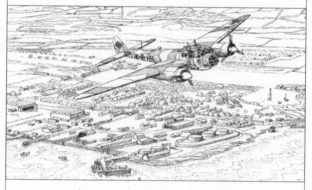

*Bombing of Pembroke Dock 1940*

I was a war child, an only child, born in 1933. International history affected my development and attitudes in many ways. Everyone in England of my generation was affected in some way by the wars of the twentieth century. Compared with many others I was fortunate. I lost no relatives and was not injured or harmed in any way by air raids of the Second World War.

I am of Irish, Welsh and Armenian descent. My father, Abgar Read Aidin (*1897-1972*), was a doctor. His Irish mother Isabella Read (*1851-1919*) trained as a nurse before going to Iran in about 1880, working for the Society for the Promoting of Female Education in the East, known as FES. My grandmother was one of the earliest single Protestant women missionaries to be sent overseas. She married an Armenian in Iran and had three children, my father and two daughters. The Armenian name Aidinjanz was anglicised to Aidin.

*Michael's grandmother Isabella Read*

My father was educated in Ireland and went to Trinity College, Dublin where he qualified as a doctor. His two sisters, Armenouhie (*1891-1981*) and Emily (*1892-1967*), were missionaries in Iran. These were bright, intelligent women both of whom lived into old age but never married. Of course, there may be many reasons which a child would not know about but I suspect it was because there was a shortage of suitable potential husbands, as over nine million men were killed overall in the First World War. Certainly, my mother had one sister who did not marry who was a school teacher in Wales. I have no doubt that aunt very much regretted being in her position. But for the conflict of the First World War, it is most likely these women would have married and had children.

*Michael, aged three, with his aunts Armenouhie and Emily*

My mother, Doris Edwards (1905-85), came from Pembroke in West Wales, where her father had worked in the naval dockyard. She trained as a pharmacist and went to work for my father in London. They married in 1929 and continued to live in London after my birth. During the 1930s my mother regularly read the US *Reader's Digest* waiting for my father to return from his nightly callouts. She would never go to sleep until he returned. She became convinced from reports of rearmament in Germany, not published in the English newspapers, that another war was inevitable.

*Michael's parents*

In 1937, my parents took me on holiday to Montreux in Switzerland. In September, the following year, we went by car to the South of France, crossing the Channel by ferry and then drove down the Route Nationale 7 to

Cannes. We stayed at the Hotel Regina, then rather smart. The Regina still exists as a bed and breakfast pension. I stayed there again for sentimental reasons, to the surprise of my colleagues, on a business trip more than fifty years later.

My parents noticed that there were few British people around. They thought it was the end of the season and anyway they had not gone to France to meet English people. They were on vacation and took no interest in the newspapers. One day they saw a newspaper headline 'Mobilisation Générale'. Their French was not good but they had heard those words before. 'General mobilisation'. They bought an English newspaper and found that Chamberlain, the prime minister, had flown to Munich and that Britain was on the verge of war with Germany.

'Always follow the international news abroad,' my father said as we immediately set off across France back to England and obtained a sea passage without difficulty, as all the other British tourists had gone home already. Some Americans who were staying in the same hotel with a child of my age congratulated my mother on her coolness and detachment. However, she was blissfully ignorant of the mounting crisis. The Americans, with no fear of U-boats, calmly arranged for a ship to take them home to Boston.

Ever since I heard the story of our flight from Cannes I have followed the news carefully when abroad.

War came in 1939. In 1940 when the bombing began in London, my mother took me to stay at her mother's home. My grandmother's house was in a part of Pembroke called Orange Gardens named after the Prince of Orange. My father worked as a doctor for the Government's Emergency Medical Service. I attended school in Stackpole where Aunt Alice, my mother's sister, was a teacher. I remember Aunt Alice and I being taken to school in the post van which at the time took passengers along with delivering parcels.

I was in Pembroke when part of the remnants of the British Army in France arrived after the evacuation at Dunkirk in 1940. I remember soldiers being quartered in extreme discomfort in Pembroke Castle as a temporary barracks. Local people donated blankets and towels. When the air raids came, we spent nights beneath the stairs with candles listening to the planes overhead. I felt alarmed but said nothing. German aircraft engines produced a slightly different beat. For some reason, this was always denied by the Air Ministry but it was well known to the population.

Pembroke seemed a nice safe place but it is close to Pembroke Dock which was then an important naval base and went on to be heavily bombed. One afternoon in August 1940, in the garden of my grandmother's house, I saw a silver aircraft flying low. An explosion shook the ground and the sky filled with black smoke – the oil tanks near Pembroke Dock had been hit, igniting thousands of tons of crude oil. Firemen were brought from Cardiff and Swansea and were unable to contain the blaze which burnt for more than eighteen days. It was the largest fire in the country since the Great Fire of London in 1666, until the London blitz.

My mother and I then moved to Lampeter in mid-Wales to avoid the bombing. There I acquired my first dog, a collie puppy we called RAF as he was born on the day the Royal Air Force claimed to have shot down one hundred and eighty German aircraft in one day in the Battle of Britain.

In 1941 air attacks on London diminished and we returned to our house there. Bombing still took place at night. In our house, we had some protection from bombing with a Morrison table supplied as air raid protection, under which one could sleep and which was supposed to be strong enough to protect one if the house collapsed. This was named after Peter Mandleson's grandfather Herbert Morrison, who was Home Secretary during Churchill's administration in the War. I saw a steel shelter of this kind at the Imperial War Museum in London, about twenty years ago.

The short cut on the way to school was across the local tennis courts. Often my friends and I found pieces of shrapnel from the anti-aircraft barrage lying on the ground. We were told not to pick up the shrapnel because it was still red hot. Probably there were fears about the risks of an explosion from a shell which had failed to detonate, but I do not remember being told about this. It seemed death was all around.

Soon my father was called up by the army and, as a doctor, was sent to West Africa because he had training in tropical medicine. He was fortunate because due to the difficulties with the climate, tours were limited to eighteen months. However, in Africa he contracted malaria which impaired his health for some years.

The bombing in Wales decreased and I returned with my mother to Pembroke. My mother bought her furniture from London which she stored in a builder's yard near her mother's home. At the end of the war, the shed was opened and nearly all the furniture turned out to be ruined by damp. My poor mother was heartbroken and it was difficult to replace the furniture with post war shortages. I think the only pieces that really survived were the Persian carpets.

I attended the local state school and I remember being in the playground in 1944 when the headmaster came out and told us the invasion of France had started.

My experience of the war was pretty sheltered. I was, of course, aware of the bombing but our house was never hit and no one close to me ever suffered. Neither was I aware of the father of any of my school contemporaries being killed or injured. I do recall hearing my mother say that a young woman who had lost her husband in the RAF went to the local bank. The teller expressed his sympathy. My mother and her friends were very cross at his insensitivity at saying anything, but I thought then, as I do now, that this was not an unreasonable human reaction.

One incident I do recall. My mother and other local people were involved in fundraising to buy an ambulance for the local hospital. Many American soldiers in 1943 and 1944 were stationed in Pembrokeshire for training on British Army facilities before the invasion of France. Americans helped with fund raising and gave generously. The money for the ambulance having been found, the hospital said that this was fine but they were not in a position to pay a crew in the days before the National Health Service. The trust which had been created for the ambulance had to be varied to allow some of the money to be used for paying a crew. For legal reasons, it was necessary to obtain the consent of the Americans who had been involved in the fund raising, as the money raised was only to be used for the purpose given. These men were approached via the US Army but the message came back that they had nearly all been killed in the liberation of France which we found very upsetting.

After the war in 1946 my parents took me on holiday to Switzerland. (Enterprising as this was in the early days in the post-war world.) We went by ferry to Calais and then on by train to Basel. The harbour at Calais was almost totally destroyed, the scene of heavy fighting both in 1940 and in 1944. The only new building was the Gare Maritime Harbour Station which had been rebuilt so international communication could be resumed.

The train to Switzerland travelled slowly, crossing many temporary military bridges at walking pace. There was no food on the train and we reached Basel, tired and hungry. Neutral Switzerland seemed like a fairyland to me with shops full of food and goods to buy, lovely cakes and patisserie and totally different from bombed and poverty-stricken France and England.

I had a splendid holiday in Weggis on the shores of Lake Lucerne. However, on the journey home I began to shiver and did not feel well: Switzerland was a personal disaster for me. Concerned for my health, my parents booked seats on the Golden Arrow, a luxury train from Dover to London. I travelled back to Britain with a high fever. In London, the hotel doctor thought I had 'flu. My father did not agree and believed I had polio. He found a distinguished neurologist called Sir Francis Walsh, who came to see me on the way to his daughter's wedding, wearing a top hat and a tail coat which I had never seen before. To me he looked like an undertaker which, with a high fever, I found alarming. He confirmed the diagnosis as polio.

I was taken by ambulance to the Infectious Diseases Hospital in Swansea. I was thirteen and I remained there for almost a year. This was spent in bed in hospital, doing exercises and resting. Polio has now been virtually eliminated with the Salk vaccine. Sixty years ago, it was a major public health problem, expected to grow with rising prosperity. President Franklin Roosevelt is probably the most famous example of someone who led an energetic life despite the disability of polio. Princess Margaret's husband, Anthony Armstrong Jones, had polio as a child.

*Michael recuperating in hospital*

My polio was probably contracted from American soldiers (with whom I was swimming in Lake Lucerne) on leave in Switzerland from the US army in Germany. There was then a polio epidemic in American soldiers in Germany and no cases were reported in Pembroke. I was told about this by a German doctor I consulted about my post-polio problems when I was living in New York.

In the end, I was fortunate. Although I had extensive paralysis, on the whole I made a good recovery. My back, arms, legs were affected but not the muscles of the chest which, if they fail, kill. I still remember a consultant coming to see me in hospital saying, 'Don't worry, old chap, of course you will walk again.' Until that moment, it had never occurred to me that I might not one day be walking. At the time, of course, I had no awareness of the strain on my parents, who understood the risks and uncertainties. Would the disease spread to the muscles of my chest so my lungs would not function? Or would the paralysis diminish or get worse? The treatment at that time was disputed – complete rest or a regime of exercise. I do not think anyone knew really which was better. I did both, some exercise and some rest – a fine British compromise.

For me, the legacy of polio was that one leg is a little shorter than the other so I walk with a slight limp. I could not run, hold a tennis racket over my shoulder and therefore could not participate in games, so important in education at the time. At school, I tried rowing but a boat is driven forward by pressure on the crossbeam and I could not kick with equal strength in both legs so no boat in which I was rowing ever ran true. Besides, I was the wrong shape for rowing; one needs to be tall and muscular.

My parents had originally arranged to send me as a boarder to Clifton, a public (private) school in Bristol. I was wearing a steel and leather back support and a steel calliper on one leg so a boarding school education was out of the question. My father found a job in Bristol so I could go as a day boy. This was not a success for him and I now realise he made a career mistake in accepting a position which did not place him well in the reorganisation of the medical service which at that time was taking place in Britain.

Clifton was difficult for me because in those days, transferring to the independent system of education from the state schools meant a change of syllabus, and public schools and the state system were very different. This was not an easy transition. Most public-school boys attended a preparatory (junior) school. I had to start learning Latin which my contemporaries had been taught at their preparatory schools since they were eight years old. Of course, I could not take part in games, and developed a resistance to the prevailing interest in sport – perhaps because I felt excluded.

More seriously I did not progress with academic work. I seemed perfectly bright but did not appear to apply myself. Long afterwards, through my children, I found out that I had a learning difficulty – dyslexia.

It was clear that I would be unfit for army service which meant there was no possibility of my ever joining the military under conscription, which was then operating in Britain. My position was different to that of almost all my contemporaries, as I knew from an early age that I would not be expected to fight. To what extent this affected my approach to war, I do not know, but I think I lacked a secret fear which must have troubled most of my contemporaries.

In my last term at Clifton, I obtained excellent 'O' level results but I was old for my class as I had missed about two years of teaching due to polio. On the strength of these results, my father wrote to Canon Robert Howard, Master of St Peter's, Oxford, who had married into a missionary family from Iran. My father had known Mrs Howard when they were children in Isfahan. Canon Howard asked me for an interview in Oxford and I was given lunch at the high table (a great honour for a schoolboy).

The Master said with a bit of luck and some good teaching I should have a sporting chance of obtaining a place at St Peter's. On Canon Howard's recommendation, I was sent to a crammer in St George's Square, Pimlico, run by a retired Eton master. I was encouraged to read history and French literature and The Spectator which I still read.

However, more disasters came. The day before the Oxford entrance examination I was taken to hospital with acute appendicitis. This was the beginning of a period of ill health with three operations during my university years. I had to take a later college entrance examination in history, French, essay writing, etc., in which I did rather well. I was given the benefit of the doubt because of the result and because of my illness, notwithstanding my deplorable results from school.

While at Oxford I developed a stone in my kidney. This was perhaps due to the nursing when I was in bed with polio. In the days when people spent long periods in bed with TB, it was well known that it was important to make the patients drink plenty of water as otherwise they often accumulated grit in their kidneys. Frequent drinking caused more work for nursing staff. In a well-run hospital, the nurses made sure patients took plenty of fluids. This did not happen in my case.

In those days, kidney stones could only be removed by major surgery. Meanwhile the condition was very painful. I stayed at Oxford for an extra year. I found being a semi-invalid in a group of active and energetic young people was stressful and depressing. One day at lunch someone said 'Roger Bannister is going to try for the four-minute mile this afternoon at the university athletic grounds. Who is coming to watch?' My friend said, 'Michael does not know where the athletic ground is', which was in fact true, but I found it distressing and I tried to laugh it off. In the event, I did not go. I regret this as I missed one of the most important events of my time at Oxford.

I had intermittent pain from the kidney stone for which I was given analgesic. A foolish doctor in Oxford encouraged me to take whatever dosage of Pethidine I needed to contain the pain. After surgery, the nurses had to be firm with me in withholding the pain killers which had ceased to be necessary. I now realise that I was close to addiction and no doubt the excessive medication harmed my work.

After I recovered from the surgery, one day I woke up with a fever and a swollen neck. At Blackwell's, the university bookshop, I looked up a basic cram book for medical students and decided my symptoms coincided with those of mumps. I saw the college doctor, who agreed, and sent me off to an isolation hospital. After a couple of days my father came to see me and said, 'You haven't got mumps, you have a swollen neck. Where is that fool of a house physician?' I had glandular fever which produced high temperatures, low energy and was a miserable thing to have at a critical time in my university career and when all my contemporaries were dynamic.

I took a degree in Law as I really could not study any other subject as my academic grounding from Clifton was insufficient. In a degree course, one learnt the legal rules and the history of law. The things in law which interested me were the Perry Mason cut and thrust in court and the use of legal drafting in drawing up documents and doing deals. These aspects of law were not part of the course and the undiagnosed learning difficulty made my academic career unsatisfactory. However, I did obtain a pretty good general education, going to many lectures outside my field: history with A.J.P. Taylor, Literature with Lord David Cecil and other lectures by Professor of Law, Cyril Falls. I remember going to a lecture he gave on 'Clauswitz on War'. I obtained a copy of the book and spent one warm afternoon reading it in the college quadrangle. I was overwhelmed by the analytical calculations of the infliction of casualties to obtain a political end.

*Michael and his Aunt Nouhie*

I remember sitting, shivering with shock. I think I can almost date my revulsion from war from that afternoon. Subsequently, after leaving university, I won a public essay competition on world government and the creation through international law of a society which would make war less common, if not outlaw it altogether. Sadly, I do not know what happened to this paper.

After leaving Oxford I decided to become an accountant. I did not want to become a lawyer because I was nervous whether my health was adequate for the stress of the work. Besides, to some extent, I had been switched off law by the Oxford course. With hindsight, one cannot think of a less suitable career than accountancy for a dyslectic. My old maths master from school, who I met at a party, spilt a glass of sherry down his trousers when I told him of my career plans.

I became involved in international tax work where basic legal knowledge was useful and numeracy was not essential. I worked in a series of stressful and demanding jobs as an international tax adviser where my knowledge of basic principles of international law was helpful. This involved constant travel, but I missed scarcely a day due to ill health. I came to the conclusion regular work obviously suited me. Perhaps this is why in my eighties, I still churn out material on my dictating machine.

I spent the last forty years of my working life as a taxation adviser and with my knowledge of fiscal issues in the extractive industries became adviser to the Thomson Corporation of Toronto when oil was discovered in the North Sea. I established reporting procedures for Thomson's oil interests, which produced a great deal of money. Thomson made substantial investments with heavy borrowings to finance their investment in the Piper and Claymore fields in North Sea Oil on a limited recourse basis. After the Piper Alpha platform disaster in 1988 when one hundred and sixty-seven men tragically lost their lives, Thomson decided to withdraw from the oil industry and concentrate on publishing.

Thomson invested in publishing in North America, and I soon found myself dealing with tax issues in the US and Canada, and eventually transferred to New York where I lived for about ten years. This was when my interest in American history and war memorials developed.

After retirement, I saw the memorials in St Petersburg, Turkey, Romania, Ireland, Pakistan and Iran as well as many British memorials in India, such as The India Gate in New Delhi.

Chance is an odd thing. One wonders what would have happened to me if I had not gone to Switzerland in 1946 and caught polio. Perhaps I would have been like the boy sitting next to me at lunch at school the day the Korean War began. Perhaps I would have found myself in the Army having an extremely unpleasant and dangerous time in Korea. He said he refused to take any interest in the war as in one hundred years' time it would be ten lines in the history book. No doubt he was correct, but he went to Korea with the Gloucestershire Regiment, a local Regiment in Bristol. I never found out what happened to him.

# ✧ Chapter Two ✧
## Itchy Feet

*Thiepval Memorial to the Missing of the Somme*

Mervyn Matthews (*1932–*) was also in hospital in Swansea with Perthes' disease, a rare disease of the hip caused by a lack of blood supply. Mervyn comes from a Swansea family where his father worked in the docks.

Mervyn is an exceptionally intelligent person. We were the only boys of about the same age in the hospital. It was not a particularly nice or efficient hospital but it pulled us through extremely trying illnesses.

After we left hospital, Mervyn and I were both rather lonely. We missed the comradeship of the hospital. We spent a fair amount of time together and Mervyn came to stay at my parents' home in Bristol as he had an aunt not far away. We have kept in touch since our stay in hospital for over seventy years.

We both had itchy feet. I remember when I was nineteen in 1952, hitch-hiking to France with Mervyn.

We hitchhiked to Southampton and took a steamer trip to Le Havre and made our way round parts of northern France and Normandy. We became more adventurous in our travels. We went to Paris and then we hitch-hiked to the South of France, making our way down to Cassis, not far away from Marseilles. We got a lift from a Canadian army officer and his wife, and ended up travelling through the night on a lorry with young white Russians (members of the White Russian Movement, a military force who fought against the Bolshevik reds for control of Russia during the Russian Civil War) – useful for Mervyn who was studying Russian at university.

I remember Mervyn's shock as I fell asleep on a beach in the South of France after sampling a bottle or two of local wine. Fortunately, we had enough money to travel back by train because northbound hitches were not easy to obtain.

Mervyn did well in school and university and ended up at Oxford where he became a junior fellow at St Anthony's College. He is a gifted linguist specialising in French and

Russian languages and as he became more fluent, started to study Russian society. I am dyslexic so in no way could compete linguistically with him.

*Michael and Mervyn*

Eventually, Mervyn made his way to Russia where he met a nice clever Russian girl called Lyudmila at the Lenin Library in Moscow.

Our paths then parted while Mervyn was in Russia. However, out of the blue I had a telephone call from the Foreign Office asking if Mervyn could stay with my parents in Worthing. My parents had been kind to Mervyn and had entertained him in our home for many years.

Mervyn was being expelled from Russia because the Russians did not approve of love affairs between foreigners and their nationals. I telephoned my mother to ask her if it would be OK for Mervyn to stay with my parents at their home in Worthing. My mother said, 'He has been in the Daily Mail every day this week.' I said I have not heard anything about Mervyn's activity as I read only the Times and Financial Times. Eventually he returned to England and I took him in my car to my parents' house in Worthing.

*Michael and Mervyn in Michael's parent's garden*

Mervyn and Mila, whom he eventually extracted from Russia and married continue to live in a house in Pimlico which they have had for many years.

\* \* \*

France has great attractions for a student of war memorials. The combination of distinguished monuments, complex history, fine scenery, a good road system, comfortable hotels and fine restaurants makes a study of memorials in France an agreeable way of exploring the follies of humanity.

Every village in France has a memorial to the men of the district who lost their lives. These are usually simple steles (stone shafts) or statues of a poilu, a French private soldier standing alone. There are also many larger, more complex monuments, some of which constitute distinguished works of art.

Most war memorials in France commemorate the one and a half million Frenchmen killed in the Great War (1914-1918). France's allies also erected many memorials to their dead. The battle zones of Eastern France on the line of the front from Switzerland to the sea have hundreds of military cemeteries and battle monuments.

The most famous monument in France is the Arc de Triomphe designed by Jean Chalgrin (*1739-1811*). Work began on the arch in 1806. It was unfinished when Napoleon fell from power but completed between 1832 and 1836 as a means of diminishing some of the post war tensions of France. The great arch is fifty metres high, forty-five metres wide and situated at a great crossroads called l'Etoile (the star) at the Place Charles de Gaulle on the brow of a hill, looking in one direction down the Champs-Elysées towards the Place de la Concorde and the Louvre and in another direction down the hill towards the Seine. Facing the Champs-Elysées there is the famous heroic group known as the Marseillaise carved by Rude, a fervent admirer of Napoleon, showing the departure of the volunteers from Paris in 1792 to oppose the invasion of Prussia and Lorraine. The Arc de Triomphe walls are lined with the names of Napoleon's battles but the British visitor will seek without success for Trafalgar and Waterloo. The names of Napoleon's Marshalls who lost their lives are inscribed on the ceiling with their names underlined.

The French Unknown Soldier was buried under the arch on 28th January 1921, with a gravestone with the simple words, 'Ici repose un soldat français mort pour la Patrie. 1914-1918.' A flame is rekindled daily. Originally it was intended to bury the unknown soldier at the Panthéon in Paris, the state burial place of the great and good of the French Republic, but in deference to public opinion the site of the grave was moved to the Arc de Triomphe.

On 11th November every year, a public holiday in France, The President of the Republic goes to the Tomb of the Unknown Soldier, to commemorate the anniversary of the ending of the First World War.

General de Gaulle proclaimed the liberation of Paris from the German occupation, at the Arc de Triomphe in August 1944.

After I retired, on holiday in Paris, I was anxious to see the parade at the Arc de Triomphe on Armistice Day. I telephoned the military attaché at the British Embassy in Paris who said, 'You would be wasting your time old boy, owing to the strict security.' I then wrote to a friend who was an international lawyer working for the French government who was able to arrange tickets for us. These arrived in a simple brown envelope and my wife and I set off and were waved fast through the police lines into the Arc de Triomphe. The officer commanding was accompanied by his aide-de-camp who was a superbly smart young French woman officer.

Memorialisation to the war dead can be a form of political protest. Certainly, in France, after the disastrous war with Prussia in 1870,

The French erected some distinguished monuments. Antonin Mercie (*1845-1916*) had won the Prix de Rome in 1870 where he was living when news of the war came. Mercie at once designed a Victory Monument showing a winged figure of Fame supporting a victorious warrior, but when he heard of the French defeat he substituted a dead or dying warrior with a broken sword. The Wings of Fame appears to have been derived from the Victory at Samothrace in the Louvre.

In about 1871 when Alsace and Lorraine were ceded to Germany, the tide turned and there was an altogether different spirit behind the memorials erected in France. The memorials were often consciously intended to stimulate national fervour and the spirit of revenge and are of limited appeal.

The many statutes of Joan of Arc erected towards the end of the nineteenth century, were intended to remind the French of their national heritage and Joan's role in driving the English from France. The parallel fact that Joan came from Lorraine, then part of Germany, would not have been lost on contemporaries. In a complex way, the statues of Joan of Arc which one sees all over France, are memorials not only to St Joan but also the French killed in 1870. Rodin, the greatest French sculptor of the period, failed to win a competition for a memorial to the dead of the city of Paris because his design was insufficiently aggressive.

The sculptor Emile Guillaume (1867-1942) was ranked by contemporaries with Rodin as one of the leading sculptors in France in the early twentieth century. La Déliverance was created to celebrate the victory of the French Army in the Battle of the Marne in 1914, when the taxis of Paris took the soldiers to the front, where they defeated the German attack on Paris.

Lord Rothermere, the press tycoon, saw a memorial called La Déliverance at an exhibition in Paris after the war and although not a conventional memorial, he bought it and presented it to Finchley, London which was in need of a war memorial. Certainly, the nude young woman grasping a sword is not the kind of art one

La Déliverance,
Finchley, London

associates with memorials of this kind.

The statue in Finchley was unveiled in 1927 by David Lloyd George, the former prime minister, who took a keener interest in it than the other war memorials he had unveiled. Lloyd George was known to be susceptible to the fairer sex. The mother-in-law of a friend of mine, worked as a land girl in a team on his farm in the Second World War. Although about eighty, Lloyd George showed his continuing interest in the opposite sex by pinching the girls' bottoms every day when they came to work.

Another version of La Déliverance was incorporated into the city war memorial at Nantes in Western France. The provocative nude shocked the relatives of the dead. The monument was vandalised and eventually removed.

The story of La Déliverance, as a war memorial both in England and France, is intriguing, and I hope someone will soon give a full account of it.

The most striking commemoration of the war dead is the hundreds of cemeteries in Belgium and France. Custom varied between different countries. The British practice was to bury the dead as close to where they fell as possible in individual graves. After collection from the battlefields, the French tended to bury their dead in giant ossuaries (places for the deposit of the bones of the dead). The ossuary at Verdun looks not unlike a London underground station. It contains the bones of hundreds of thousands of dead soldiers collected from the battlefield in the First World War. One suspects that the French were unable to distinguish in many cases whether they were French or Germans so they are therefore all mixed up.

Many British people visit these cemeteries, often in school parties, so they make a great impression on the collective memory of the public. The British suffered large casualties in the attack on the Germans at the Somme in 1916. Many bodies could not be found. In the 1960s, my parents had a friend in Worthing, a retired teacher from Manchester who still wore the engagement ring she had been given by her fiancée who was killed on the Somme.

Edwin Lutyens (*1869-1944*), a favourite architect of mine, was commissioned to design a monumental arch with sufficient spaces to list the names of all the British missing. This he achieved through a series of interlocking arches in one monument. The memorial to the Missing of the Somme at Thiepval is one of the great memorials of the world. I once approached the monument early on an autumn morning to find it appearing as a ghostly shape through the mist rising from the river.

On another occasion, I was at a conference in 1996 commemorating the eightieth anniversary of the Battle of the Somme for a ceremonial rededication of the monument by the Duke of Gloucester, with the British Ambassador and many British and French dignitaries. Participants of the conference were being taken on a bus to the ceremony. My wife and I were a few minutes late, or perhaps the bus left a few minutes early. Waiting by our car, wondering what to do, a French Professor from Paris arrived and was very cross to find he had been left behind. He said, 'Follow me,' and drove off at alarming speed. When we arrived at the monument it was surrounded with security police. Our friend drove up, shouted at the policemen and was waved through. My wife, in her best French, said, 'We are with that gentleman.' The police saluted smartly and we passed through.

Perhaps the most poignant American monument in France is that to former president Theodore Roosevelt's son Quentin. At a party,

Quentin met a clever, beautiful young girl called Flora Vanderbilt Whitney. Her father was a Whitney and her mother a Vanderbilt, both from the richest families in America. The couple fell in love and became informally engaged. The Roosevelts were enchanted with Flora, but they were old money and rather staid. The Whitneys were rather fast. Flora's mother, Gertrude, was a talented sculptor and a considerable organiser who had taken a hospital to France before America entered the war.

Gertrude's old bedroom, at the family home at Providence, Rhode Island, contains models of some of the important sculptures for which she was responsible. This includes the monument at St Nazaire, the port used by disembarking American troops upon arrival in France. This monument was destroyed in the Second World War by the Germans who wanted the metal but it was rebuilt identically by Pierre Fouesnant in 1989 at the same location on the beach of Grand Traict.

When he arrived in France, Quentin was found to be one of only two American officers who could speak good French. With his charm and contacts, he was engaged on liaison duties. He had two brothers serving in France and his sister was married to an Army Medical Officer. However, he wished to be assigned to flying duties and, on 14th July 1918, was shot down.

Roosevelt, a regular correspondent of Rudyard Kipling, had encouraged his underage son with poor eyesight to enlist. When the boy was killed, Roosevelt was devastated by the loss and felt intense regret that he had encouraged his son to go to France. A few days after the news was received a maid found Roosevelt alone in his bedroom, moving back and forth in a rocking chair on which he had nursed all his children, muttering to himself over and over again, 'Poor Quentikins, poor Quentikins.'

Responding to a message of sympathy from King George V, Roosevelt wrote:

*'Your Majesty, it was very kind and thoughtful of Her Majesty the Queen, and you, Sir, to cable us about the death of our son Quentin; and Mrs Roosevelt and I thank you both, with all our hearts. Of his three brothers Ted, who is a Major of Infantry, has been gassed once and is now in hospital with a bullet through his leg; Archie, a Captain of Infantry, has been badly wounded by a shell; both were cited for gallantry, in orders; Kermit has been Captain of an armored machine gun motor battery with your army in Mesopotamia, has been given the Military Cross, and is now with*

*our army under Pershing. Unlike most of their fellow-countrymen they had prepared in advance! They sailed from our shores over a year ago; their mother and I knew their temper and quality; and we did not expect to see all of them come back.'* [1]

Quentin's body was moved to the American Military Cemetery in Normandy after the Second World War, where he lies in a grave next to that of his brother, Theodore (Ted). Ted was awarded the Medal of Honor for bravery in the D-Day landings in 1944.

In February 1919, Quentin's mother went to Chamery, France to arrange for a memorial at the village where he was shot down. The monument designed by Paul Cret (*1876-1945*) consists of a sandstone fountain carved with United States and French emblems with a tiger head symbol. Cret was a French National trained in the Beaux Arts tradition who, in the early years of the twentieth century, had achieved great professional success in the United States. In 1914, he joined the French Forces and remained in France during the war. Subsequently he became consulting architect to the American Battle Monuments Commission.

Theodore Roosevelt desired a monument which would be useful to the village and contributed $7,000 from the Nobel Peace Prize which he had received for his work in the negotiations which ended the Russo-Japanese war in 1905.

*Memorial to Quentin Roosevelt, Chamery, France*

Cret in a newspaper interview in 1919 said, 'If you have not been in France, you do not know how important the village fountain is. It is usually the sole source of water supply in small towns. The women bring their buckets and pitchers to be filled at the place each day. Once or twice a week they bring their family washing and do it there, and each night the cattle are driven up for their drinks.' It was also the exchange point of the village for local gossip and news.

\* \* \*

The memorial to Lieutenant George Cecil (*1895-1914*) by François-Leon Sicard (*1862-1934*) is one of the finest private monuments erected on the Western Front. Situated in the woods at Villers-Cotterêts, about twenty miles from Compiègne, the monument is close to a small cemetery containing about a hundred graves of officers and men of the Grenadier, Coldstream and Irish Guards killed on 1st September 1914. Rudyard Kipling in his *Irish Guards in the Great War* wrote, 'perhaps the most beautiful of all resting-places in France, on a slope of the forest off the dim road, near the Rond de la Reine, holds our dead in that action.' [2]

Although the monument is fine, the story behind it is particularly interesting. Why was such a distinguished monument put up to one of the millions of the young men killed in France in what, to the British, is the most terrible of all wars?

The Cecil monument consists of a statue of a woman dressed in the style of Ancient Greece, studying a stone carving on what may be the grave of a soldier. Sicard, winner of the Prix de Rome in 1891, was a well-known French sculptor of the period. Probably his most famous war memorial work is the Archibald Fountain in Sydney, Australia. He also executed important memorials in France at Blois and Fécamp. The statue is similar to that known as the Mourning Athene from the Acropolis in Athens. Traditionally, this was considered to be the goddess Athene studying the list of the Athenian dead from the Battle of Marathon in 498 BC. Here the figure, leaning on a pilgrim staff, is studying a contemporary army helmet, presumably on the grave of someone dear to her.

George Cecil was a grandson of the third Marquis of Salisbury, three times prime minster. Of his ten grandsons, George was one of five who were killed in the war and was the only son of Lord and Lady Edward Cecil. Lord Edward Cecil started life as a soldier, a Grenadier, and later became an official in the British civil service in Egypt. Lady Edward was born Violet Maxse, the daughter of Admiral Maxse, a hero of the Crimean War and a well-known atheist and radical. Her brother, General Sir Ivor Maxse, became Inspector of Training in the Great War. Violet had been brought up by her father (her parents were separated), partly in Paris, where she had studied art and music, and she knew many prominent people including Degas, Rodin and Georges Clemenceau. Violet was a clever and intrepid young woman. She climbed the Eiffel Tower while it was under construction, not the act of a conventional girl in Victorian times. In 1932, on the death of her brother Leo, Violet took over the editorship of the National Review, a political journal, and retained the position until 1948.

George Cecil was still only eighteen when he went to France on 13th August 1914 with his father's old regiment. The Grenadiers were involved in heavy fighting in the forest near Villers-Cotterêts. On 1st September, George Cecil was killed, sword in hand, leading a bayonet charge.

First reports were that Cecil had been wounded and taken prisoner. Elaborate enquiries were made about his fate. One can see the British class and social system of the period in operation. Rudyard Kipling, who was a neighbour of the Cecils in Sussex, questioned British soldiers who had survived the battle for news of George Cecil. Lord Milner, whom Violet Cecil married after her husband's death, and who spoke fluent German, interrogated prisoners-of-war. The American Ambassador in Berlin made enquiries of the German authorities arranged for by Lord Kitchener. When no information was forthcoming, Lady Edward decided to go to France to make enquiries on the spot and Clemenceau, The French prime minister, sent a series of telegrams authorising her to enter a military zone as fighting was still taking place not too far away. Lady Edward went to Villers-Cotterêts in the American ambassador's car later in September, escorted by his military attaché. Although a communal grave dug by the German Army had been found in the forest, this expedition did not produce any firm information.

In November 1914 Lord Killanin (brother of Colonel Morris of the Irish Guards who had been killed in the fight) went with Lord Robert Cecil MP, uncle of George Cecil, who was working for the Missing and Wounded Department of the Red Cross, Lord Elphinstone and an English clergyman from Paris, to find the remains of the men who had died. The communal grave was opened. The bodies of four officers and ninety-four men were found and the bodies of most, including George, were identified. In view of the time since burial and the wounds on the bodies, this was a gruesome and distressing task. The men were reburied in the forest. Coffins were obtained for the bodies of the officers. These were conveyed to the cemetery at Villers-Cotterêts. A funeral service, attended by the Mayor of Villers-Cotterêts, other civil officials, a French Colonel and some twenty French soldiers, took place. There was a constant background noise of artillery fire from the Front, not far away on the Aisne. Lord Killanin was asked to follow the French custom, and, as a relative of the deceased stand at the entrance of the cemetery, and as those who had attended the funeral passed out to shake hands with them and to thank them for having come. Lord Killanin reported that the French made many most kind and touching remarks and said their presence was the least they could do to honour the brave English officers who had fought and died in their country in the common cause.

With the identification of George's body, Lady Edward's last hope disappeared. A telegram from the Kiplings said, 'We are thinking of you always and desolate to think that we can no longer help. Rudyard and Carrie.' [3]

In 1915, the Cecil Rifle Range was opened by Rudyard Kipling as a memorial at Winchester College, George's old school. Rudyard Kipling fired the first shot and scored a bulls-eye, and was enthusiastically cheered by the boys. (This seems a considerable achievement for a man with poor eyesight, who had to wear strong spectacles.) Kipling, in his speech, said to the boys:

*'You have seen and realised the very things which young Cecil felt would befall. As far as his short life allowed he ordered himself so that he might not be overwhelmed by them when they were upon him. He died – as many of you too will die – but he died knowing the issues for which he died. It is well to die for one's country. But that is not enough. It is also necessary that as long as he lives a man should give to his country, as George Cecil gave, a mind and a soul neither ignorant nor inadequate.'* (4)

George Cecil had been given a crucifix at his confirmation by his uncle Lord Hugh Cecil (later Provost of Eton) on which after his death his father had engraved the triumphant epitaph, 'Died for his country on 1st September 1914 near Villers-Cotterêts in France having continued Christ's faithful soldier and servant until his life's end.'

Twenty years later Violet gave a sixteenth century painting of the Crucifixion to the chapel at Hatfield House in memory of George and his father.

*Cecil Monument, Villers-Cotterêts, France*

In 1922, the monument at Villers-Cotterêts was erected. After the war, the bodies of the officers and men were reburied in a British military cemetery close to the Cecil monument. Gravestones were placed on the inside of the wall surrounding the cemetery. On the gravestones, one sees some of the most famous names of the British aristocracy – a Cecil, a Lambton (grandson of the Earl of Durham) and that of Colonel Morris, Lord Killanin's brother.

When I visited the cemetery, I found a note from the present Lord Killanin (the distinguished Irish film producer, Redmond Morris) saying he had come from Dublin to visit his grandfather's grave.

The photograph of the monument was taken by Dillon Bryden, a professional photographer, and great grandson of Colonel Morris.

The inscription below the statue reads 'Passant, arrête-toi', words from a poem by La Fontaine which may be translated as 'Stop, you who pass by.' On the reverse side, the following is carved:

'IN HONOUR OF THE OFFICERS AND MEN OF THE GRENADIER, COLDSTREAM AND IRISH GUARDS WHO FELL NEAR THIS SPOT ON 1st SEPTEMBER 1914. THIS MEMORIAL WAS PLACED HERE BY THE MOTHER OF ONE OF THEM, AND IS ESPECIALLY DEDICATED TO SECOND LIEUTENANT GEORGE EDWARD CECIL.'

This little cemetery encapsulates the tragedy of 1914 for Britain, for its Empire and for its ruling class. Lady Edward, until she became very old, made a pilgrimage to Villers-Cotterêts every year except during the war years of 1941-44.

A portrait of George Cecil as a boy by John Singer Sargent hangs in the Musée Clemenceau at Clemenceau's flat at 8, rue Franklin in Paris. Clemenceau befriended George when he visited Paris as a schoolboy.

Thus, several individuals were commemorated in a number of places and in many different ways. One wonders how many of the tourists who pause on the roadside at the monument in the Forêt de Retz, or who see Sargent's portrait of George Cecil in Clemenceau's flat in Paris, know the whole background.

# ✧ Chapter Three ✧
# American Dream

*The Alamo*

During my time in the United States, I was lucky enough to travel the country and discovered many memorials to the war dead. In the early 1960s, during my first job and after we had been to France, Mervyn won a scholarship while he was a post-graduate student at Harvard 'to see America' and with great kindness gave me the opportunity of going with him on what proved to be a memorable journey from coast to coast.

My parents felt that if Mervyn could cope with the Russian secret police he could cope with anything and look after me well, which he did.

We drove across the country from Cambridge, Massachusetts, by way of Chicago, to San Francisco, and then south to Flagstaff, Arizona.

On our first day, our Chevrolet car broke down in a small village in New England. While Mervyn went to look for help, I stayed with the car to guard the luggage. We had stopped on the village green by the local war memorial. Typically, this consisted of a statue of a lone soldier standing on a plinth and was one of the many thousands of mass-produced Civil War memorials. Any student of American history begins by investigating the Civil War first.

The earliest burials were simple. As the war progressed, a wooden headboard was placed at each grave identifying the deceased. After peace was made, the War Department re-interred the dead who had been buried in the battlefields or had died in prisoner-of-war camps or in hospital. White wooden headboards were placed on more than three hundred thousand graves. Marble and granite markers replaced the wooden markers early in the 1870s, when Congress decided to maintain battlefield cemeteries in perpetuity and to provide burial to all who had taken part in the War in National Cemeteries located in different parts of the United States.

Men killed in the Battle of Gettysburg, who had been buried temporarily in shallow graves, were often disinterred by local people.

Sometimes the bodies were able to be identified from items found in the men's pockets and then they were re-buried in marked graves.

The Civil War coincided with the development of the out-of-town cemetery movement in the United States. With the increased size of cities and the development of railways, it became feasible for communities to dispose of their dead in cemeteries away from city centres, thus reducing the pressure on overcrowded burial grounds. Along the lines of the early nineteenth century cemeteries surrounding Paris, such as Père La Chaise, many of these cemeteries became places where families often went for Sunday afternoon walks. This fulfilled an important Victorian death ritual and enabled the families to contemplate the memorials to the departed.

The US Government's decision to create cemeteries with, wherever possible, individual graves for men who died on the battlefield or in hospital, was an unprecedented act in the history of war. The Soldiers' National Cemetery at Gettysburg was designed in a semicircle of graves around a central monument to all the Union dead. States were given sections around the semicircle in accordance with the number of their dead. Each grave was marked with a nine-inch-high granite gravestone bearing the name, company and regiment of the deceased.

Abraham Lincoln's dedication of the cemetery at Gettysburg in 1863 is probably the most famous speech in the English language. He said:

*'Four score and seven years ago our fathers brought forth on this continent a new nation, conceived in liberty, and dedicated to the proposition that all men are created equal.*

*'Now we are engaged in a great civil war, testing whether that nation, or any nation so conceived and so dedicated, can long endure. We are met on a great battlefield of that war. We have come to dedicate a portion of that field, as a final resting place for those who here gave their lives that that nation might live. It is altogether fitting and proper that we should do this.'*

Reading Lincoln's speech today, one must remember that the war was still raging. His words, succinct, respectful, musical and reassuring, had to maintain the unity and determination of the people of the North to continue the conflict.

But Lincoln's contention that 'the world will little note nor long remember what we said here but it can never forget what they did here' was mistaken. The story of the Battle of Gettysburg will gradually fade into the darker recesses of military history, while Lincoln's speech will last until the end of history. His words rank with Churchill's radio broadcasts, Martin Luther King's call to unity, and those of Pericles, spoken at the funeral of the Athenians killed in battle early in the fifth century BC.

Waiting for Mervyn, I noticed the names engraved on the base of the memorial. The names of the Civil War dead were English, Scots or Irish. By the time of the First World War, German and other Central European names had appeared. Among the dead of the Korean War there were Hispanic names. The Vietnam War was in progress at the time of my visit but if I were to go back to the memorial I would expect, even in rural America, to find a sprinkling of Asian names among the men killed in Vietnam. Thus, one can trace the waves of immigration into the United States by looking at the names on a simple village war memorial.

Yet one should be cautious about accepting war memorials as an accurate historic record. Memorials are nearly always erected by victors and reflect their perception of history or what they hoped history will say about them. The defeated erected few memorials. Even if the vanquished are permitted to erect memorials, the views expressed may be limited by what can be said politically. For example, references to Yankee oppression, although perhaps the true sentiments in the Deep South after the Civil War would not have been tolerated on war memorials.

The only British monument I have seen to the Revolutionary War is to Major John André (*1750-1780*) who was Adjutant General to the British Army in North America. André was hanged as a spy by the Americans in 1780. A memorial designed by Robert Adam (*1728-1792*) was presented to Westminster Abbey by King George III.

*Memorial to Major André,*
*Westminster Abbey, London*

In 1818, the repatriation of his body was arranged by the British Consul in New York who, assisted by an undertaker, exhumed André's remains at Tappansee near New York, for removal to England. The local Irish, then as now strongly anti-British, resented the removal of André's body. The Consul said he was Irish himself and that in Ireland if they had to do a difficult job of this kind, they found it easier if they had a few drinks first. The Consul arranged for the local ale house to serve free beer. While the party was in progress, André's remains, still recognisable from the dress uniform in which he had been hanged, were exhumed and taken to New York to be shipped to London where they were buried in Westminster Abbey close to his monument.

The Alamo, San Antonio, Texas, is the site of a legendary battle in 1836, between the Government of Mexico and the American settlers who came from Texas. Part of the old mission complex was used as headquarters for a Spanish cavalry unit – soldiers garrisoned there named it *alamo* (cottonwood) after their base in Alamo de Parras in Mexico.

Colonisers came in search of wealth and adventure and realized money could be made in

Mexico's cotton industry. Although banned in Mexico, slavery resolved the labour problem. The battle of the Alamo was fought over issues such as slavery, immigration rights, the cotton industry and above all, money. The desperate defence of the Alamo by a small group of Texans against overwhelming odds has become part of American national folk memory.

Colonel Travis, the besieged Texan commander of the garrison, sent a letter out by messenger after dark:

*'To the people of Texas and all the Americans in the world, fellow citizens and compatriots – I am besieged by a thousand or more of the Mexicans under Santa Ana – I have sustained continual Bombardment and cannonade for twenty-four hours and have not lost a man – The enemy has demanded a surrender at discretion, otherwise, the garrison are to be put to the sword, if the fort is taken – I have answered the demand with a cannon shot, and our flag still waves proudly from the walls – I shall never surrender or retreat. Then I call on you in the name of Liberty, of patriotism and everything dear to the American character to come to our aid, with all dispatch – the enemy (is) receiving reinforcements daily and will no doubt increase to three or four thousand in four or five days. If this call is neglected, I am determined to*

*sustain myself as long as possible and die like a soldier who never forgets what is due to his duty and honor to that of his country – VICTORY OR DEATH.'*

Travis assembled his men when it became apparent that no relief would arrive, and told them that if they remained they would die. Travis pulled his sword and used it to draw a line in the ground at the Alamo. He said anyone should cross it who was not prepared to die. The legend is that all but one of the defenders, including Jim Bowie and Davy Crockett, remained with Travis on his side of the line, understanding the decision was irreversible. Only one defender, Moses Rose, chose to leave the compound. 'A line in the sand' is the phrase most commonly associated with Texas history in the United States.

Mexican soldiers breached the north wall in a final attack before dawn on 6th March, 1836. The Texan defenders made a last stand at the old church in a battle lasting about ninety minutes. The Alamo is now preserved as their memorial. To this day, the Alamo is evoked as a term of encouragement, to carry on in the face of desperate odds.

A Texas force overwhelmingly defeated the Mexicans shortly afterwards, at San Jacinto about twenty miles south east of Houston. To commemorate the centenary of the battle, an octagonal stone tower was erected in 1936, rising five hundred and seventy feet above the battlefield surmounted by the Lone Star of the State of Texas. The San Jacinto tower is very much a monument to the battle not to those killed in it, unlike the Alamo. Part of the inscription on the tower reads:

'With the battle cry, "Remember the Alamo! Remember Goliad!" (where Texan prisoners were executed in the Battle of Goliad) the Texans charged. The enemy taken by surprise, rallied for a few minutes then fled in disorder. The Texans had asked no quarter and gave none. The slaughter was appalling, victory complete, and Texas free! On the following day, General Antonio Lopez De Santa Anna, self-styled 'Napoleon of the West,' received from a generous foe the mercy he had denied Travis at the Alamo and Fannin at Goliad ...

'... Measured by its results, San Jacinto was one of the decisive battles of the world. The freedom of Texas from Mexico won here led to annexation and to the Mexican–American War, resulting in the acquisition by the United States of the states of Texas, New Mexico, Arizona, Nevada, California, Utah and parts of Colorado, Wyoming, Kansas and Oklahoma. Almost one third of the present *area of the American Nation, nearly a million square miles of territory, changed sovereignty.'*

General Phillip Kearney (*1815-1862*) was probably the most famous soldier in the United States in the nineteenth century noted for his bravery and was memorialised by two of the most famous sculptors of the nineteenth century. Henry Kirk Brown produced a statue of Kearney which stands in New Jersey and Edward Clark Potter 'a prominent animalier' (sculptor of animals), an equestrian statue which can be found in Arlington.

*Michael in front of General Kearney, Arlington*

Born into a rich New York family, Kearney reluctantly studied law at Columbia University, but his ambition was to study at West Point Military Academy. In 1836, he inherited more than a million dollars (about twenty-five million dollars today), from his grandfather. He joined the army and served in Indian Territory on the Western frontier. By 1839, Kearney had studied military tactics in France and by 1840 was aide-de-camp to American General Winfield Scott in the Mexican War.

While leading a charge his left arm was shattered by grape shot and had to be amputated. Kearney resigned his commission. He returned to France and joined the Imperial Guard of the French army. He took part in every cavalry charge at the battles of Solferino and Magenta in the Italian campaign, riding with his sword in his right hand and the reins of his horse in his mouth. He was awarded the Légion d'Honneur by Napoleon III.

At the outbreak of the Civil War, Kearney returned home and re-joined the army, despite his disabilities. He fought in numerous battles but he was killed as he tried to fight his way out, when he was cut off on a reconnaissance mission behind enemy lines at Chantilly in Virginia.

General Lee, who had known Kearney in the Mexican War, ordered his remains to be returned with his horse, saddle and equipment, to Union Lines under a flag of truce. Kearney's horse and equipment were strictly the property of the Confederacy as war booty, but Lee paid for these out of his own funds. Kearney's body was buried at Trinity Church in New York, then the most prominent church in the city. In 1912, his body was reburied at Arlington Cemetery in the presence of President Taft. Two years later, in the presence of President Woodrow Wilson, his body was reinterred at Arlington under an equestrian statue by Edward Clark Potter. The inscription of Kearney's memorial reads: *'Gave his left arm at Churubusco, Mexico, August 1847 and his life at Chantilly, Virginia, September 1862.'*

Thomas Jonathan Jackson (*1824-1863*) was one of the most gifted cavalry commanders of his day. Modern historians refer to Jackson as showing great daring, tactical skill and energy. 'There is Jackson standing like a stone wall,' a fellow general at the Battle of Manassas said, and Jackson was 'Stonewall' from that day forth. His death on May 10th, 1863, from pneumonia at the age of thirty-nine following a wound caused by friendly fire, was an irreparable loss for the Confederacy.

The story of Jackson, is best told by Stephen Vincent Benét in John's Brown's Body (published in 1928) describing how Jackson, after having his arm cut off, lay dying for four days.

There are many statues to Jackson throughout the Confederacy but the statue commissioned by a British group of sympathisers from John Henry Foley (1818-1874), captured the 'thoroughly soldier-like carriage and physique, the sagacity and indication of heroic capabilities and fortitude' as reported in the *Illustrated London News*. Foley was the most famous Irish sculptor of his time. Coutts Bank held the 'Stonewall Jackson memorial Account' which listed one hundred and fourteen individuals, two firms and a few anonymous donors. The statue is the only memorial in the Confederacy paid for with British money and it was in fact, the first statue erected in honour of a fallen Confederate hero. The inscription reads:

*'Presented by English Gentlemen*
*as a tribute of admiration for*
*the soldier and patriot*
*Thomas J Jackson*

*and gratefully accepted by Virginia*
*in the name of the southern people*
*done A.D. 1875*
*in the Hundredth year of the Commonwealth.*
*'Look! There is Jackson standing like*
*a stonewall.'*

Southerners have for a long time wondered whether the war would have ended differently had Jackson survived to fight at Gettysburg. His discipline and tactical sense were missed by General Lee.

The memorial by Augustus Saint-Guadens (1848-1907) to Colonel Robert Shaw (1837-63) and his African-American infantry is perhaps the most important memorial to those who lost their lives in the American Civil War.

Shaw raised a regiment of African-Americans to fight for the Union in the Civil War. All the soldiers faced execution if taken prisoner by the Confederate States, which did not extend the laws of war to African-Americans.

Before Union forces could capture Charleston, South Carolina, they first had to take Fort Wagner, a beach head fortification held by the Confederates that covered the southern approach to Charleston Harbour in

South Carolina. The 54th would spearhead a three-pronged attack aimed at capturing the necklace of heavily fortified islands that dotted Charleston harbour. If they could take Fort Wagner, the Federals would launch a major assault on nearby Fort Sumter. From there, it would only be a matter of time before Charleston fell. But capturing Fort Wagner was no easy task. On July 18th, 1863, Shaw, and the majority of his men, lost their lives in an attack on the Confederate Fort Wagner. The bravery of the 54th was widely reported, and this courage resulted in the Union accepting thousands of African-American men for combat. This was credited by Lincoln as helping to 'turn the tide' in the war.

Examination of war memorials raises many questions. For example, who chose the design? How many people were involved in the project? Often designers were chosen from public competitions, the results were frequently the lowest common denominator of public taste of the period. By contrast, most of the funding for this fine monument came from Shaw's wealthy abolitionist Boston family who were able to impose their wishes – without their influence the memorial might never have been erected.

*Monument to General Shaw, Boston*

Shaw, on horseback, is depicted by a bronze bas-relief, leading his marching soldiers, the 54th Massachusetts Regiment. He holds a sword in his right hand in salute to the Governor of Massachusetts in the State House of Boston. An allegorical female figure above holds a laurel or olive branch and poppies, symbolic of peace, sleep, death, remembrance and victory. Above her, an arched star-spotted ceiling is part of an elaborate stone frame marking off the carving at the back of the monument. The architectural setting was designed by the architectural firm prominent at the turn of the twentieth century, McKim, Meade & White, whose works included The Brooklyn Museum in New York and the Boston Public Library. The complex includes stone benches on both sides, and is set in a grove of trees facing the state house, the eighteenth century building which houses the government of the state of Massachusetts.

In the 1990s, I came across a remarkable monument in the form of a bronze replica of a mid-nineteenth century railway locomotive erected by the State of Ohio.

In 1862, a group of soldiers from the North led by James Andrews, seized a railway engine called 'The General' in an attempt to destroy the railway link critical to southern communications between Atlanta, Georgia and Chattanooga, Tennessee. The daring raiders who seized the locomotive, not unlike the Great British Train Robbery, were caught and eight of the men were tried as spies and hanged. Their bodies are buried at the foot of the monument. Four were among the first posthumous recipients of the Medal of Honour, so important was the event in the collective national consciousness.

*Replica of 'The General' Locomotive Chattanooga*

Chattanooga, is a typical Civil War battlefield cemetery, constructed to accommodate those killed in fiercely-fought local battles in 1863 and still in use for burials of service personnel. Typical, that is, but for the replica of 'the General'; the original is now housed at the museum of the raid, the Kennesaw Civil War Museum at Kennesaw, Georgia.

The cemetery also accommodates nearly thirteen thousand men who died in the battle of Chickamauga and Chattanooga in 1863. The battle area became the first National Military Park. There is a seven-mile self-guiding auditory tour and a visitor centre provided by the National Park Service, where the complexities of the fighting are explained, as well as the symbolism of the memorials. A furled flag, for example, indicates defeat (Confederate) and an unfurled flag victory (Union).

The story of the Great Locomotive Chase is told dramatically by John Buchan, the author of *The Thirty-Nine Steps*, in his account of the incident. Two famous films, *The General*, a 1926 American silent film starring Buster Keaton and Disney's *The Great Locomotive Chase* (1956) also captured the event.

The model of the then fifty-year-old railway locomotive is almost certainly, using the words with caution, unique among war memorials.

The National Cemetery at Arlington, the most famous military cemetery in the world, is an American shrine and a major tourist attraction, with more than three million visitors per annum. It is arranged on a hillside with spectacular views over the Potomac River towards Washington D.C.

In addition to service personnel of all ranks, several presidents are buried there. Probably the most visited grave is that of John F. Kennedy (*1917-63*) who was assassinated in Dallas, Texas. Kennedy is buried with his wife and infant children. He was entitled to his place in the cemetery due to his service in the Navy and as President, he was Commander-in-Chief.

William Howard Taft (*1857-1930*) was the only person to have been both President and Chief Justice of the United States and is buried at Arlington. Oliver Wendell Holmes (*1841-1935*), the famous jurist and Supreme Court Judge, was intensely proud of his service as a young officer in the Union army in the American Civil War was also buried at Arlington as was General Arthur MacArthur, father of General Douglas MacArthur, US Commander in the Pacific. Arthur MacArthur won the Medal of Honor for gallantry in the Civil War and his son the same decoration in the Second World War, the first father and son to be awarded the medal. The Medal of Honor is the highest military award for bravery that can be presented to an individual in the name of the Congress. Graves of recipients of the Medal have words inscribed in gold leaf. Robert Kennedy, the assassinated brother of President Kennedy, is also buried in a tomb designed by I. M. Pei (*1917–*), the famous Chinese-American architect responsible for the pyramids at the Louvre in Paris.

*Tomb of the Unknown Soldier, Arlington*

In homage to the anonymous dead of America's wars of the twentieth century, a series of tombs to unknown soldiers can be seen. The graves are protected by a superlatively smart and well-trained Guard of Honor, changing guard ceremoniously every thirty minutes. The Guard of Honor contrasts with the grave of Britain's Unknown Soldier in Westminster Abbey protected by the Abbey vergers and the Arc de Triomphe with a Paris policeman to protect the French Unknown Soldier. Before the reunification of Germany, the tomb of the German Unknown Soldier in East Berlin was protected by an East German Guard of Honor that goose-stepped with great panache and in uniforms similar to those worn by the German Army in the Second World War. The style at Arlington is similar, except without the goose-stepping.

Arlington is still a working cemetery with funerals on most days. In accordance with military protocol depending on the rank of the deceased, there may be a horse-drawn caisson (a two-wheeled vehicle for ammunition) and a rifle fusilade. In January 2000, the remains of helicopter crew lost in Vietnam nearly thirty years before were brought to Arlington for burial accompanied by a helicopter fly-past.

Pressure on space in the cemetery is restricting burials, and columbaria (place for cinerary urns) have been built where the ashes of cremated veterans are deposited.

Following the end of the Second World War, after the division of Korea, two new states had formed on the peninsula. In the north, the communist dictator Kim Il Sung (1912-94) enjoyed the support of the Soviets. In the south, the anti-communist dictator Syngman Rhee (1875-1965) enjoyed the support of the American government. Border skirmishes were common as neither dictator was content to remain on his side of the thirty-eighth parallel. Before the war even began, nearly ten thousand North and South Korean soldiers were killed in battle.

A combined Chinese and North Korean Army, aided by the Russians, invaded South Korea in June 1950. This invasion was the first military action of the Cold War. By July, American troops had entered the war on South Korea's behalf. As far as American officials were concerned, this was not simply a border dispute between two unstable dictatorships on the other side of the globe. Instead, many feared it was the first step in a communist campaign to take over the world. The war ended with an armistice in 1953.

The war, in which the US lost fifty-four thousand soldiers, was not popular in the US, and as such there are few memorials. The 1995 Korean War Memorial erected in Washington DC conveys huge emotional power and deserves special mention for its potent, unearthly atmosphere, particularly unsettling when lamp-lit at night.

Designed by Frank Gaylord (1925–) and Louis Nelson (1936–), the memorial consists of a group of ghostly figures crossing a bleak landscape in capes, giving a sense of the climate in Korea, as well as the sense of disorientation, and perhaps even the perceived arbitrariness of the war itself. The figures are representatives of different ranks, military functions and ethnic backgrounds.

*The Korean War Memorial, Washington*

Towards the end of the last century, memorials showed a different approach which did not disguise the reality of war. The Vietnam War was fought largely by conscripts, mostly from minority groups in the United States; African-Americans, Hispanics and the white underclasses. Avoiding the draft was not difficult for the educated or wealthy – former President Clinton, and President Trump undertook no military service. Their choices have been criticised but one can question whether it is really unpatriotic to avoid military service in a war which has been objected to so roundly and conscientiously.

The Commemoration Wall in Washington to Americans killed or missing in Vietnam between 1955-75 is – in style, size and association – the most remarkable war memorial in the United States and perhaps in the world. The Wall has become the most visited monument in America. It is estimated that nearly twenty million visitors (about one in ten Americans) have visited the wall since its completion in 1982.

The monumental complex itself is an object of great beauty. The monument was selected by survivors of the American service personnel for whom it has a cathartic effect, and continues to help them to come to terms with the emotional and psychological impact of the war.

*Vietnam Veterans Memorial Wall*

Unlike other memorials in Washington, it was not officially sponsored. Instead, a group of Vietnam veterans raised the funds and negotiated for a site in the mall. The ex-servicemen's requirement was that it should contain the names of all who died, make no political statement, and be harmonious with the site. The design was chosen in an architectural competition won by Maya Lin (1959–), a twenty-one-year-old Chinese American undergraduate student of architecture at Yale University. It consists of two long, black marble walls meeting at one hundred and twenty-five-degree angle and faced with reflecting black marble. The names of those lost are engraved on the marble in order of date of death, which avoids the racial bunching inevitable with an alphabetical listing. There is no record of rank, unit, origin or place of death.

Today the wall has become a depository for mementos in the form of artefacts, notes and gifts by veterans, from loved ones and the public. One woman left a wedding ring inherited from her husband who was killed in Vietnam and which she deposited the day before she remarried. Every day, staff of the National Parks Service collect and store these objects. Originally the Parks Service, responsible for maintenance, expected to clear away litter but soon realised that people were leaving items of great sentimental and emotional importance. Although carefully stored, the artefacts are almost impossible to classify. Taking rubbings of the names is also a popular way of remembering those listed.

Maya Lin's design, by its refusal to glorify war, is an implicitly pacifist work. On completion, it produced a strong reaction from members of the military establishment, as well as more conventional thinkers such as Ross Perot, who was an independent presidential candidate in 1992. The veterans accepted the pressure for a more conventional Vietnam memorial, especially since they risked being denied the site in the Mall. Two years after the wall was built, the conventional design of a group of three soldiers of different racial backgrounds by Frederick Hart (*1943-99*), was added.

*Three Servicemen Memorial*

Close to the wall a group sculpture by Glena Goodacre (*1939–*) has been erected, showing a nurse holding a soldier in her arms, an African-American woman comforting the nurse and looking at the sky, presumably awaiting a rescue helicopter, and a third woman kneeling over medical equipment. The group is surrounded by eight trees commemorating the women who are known to have died in Vietnam.

*Vietnam Women's Memorial*

'*My desire to create a lasting tribute to the American women serving in Vietnam is founded upon my deep respect for each of them, and my heartfelt payer for their "healing and hope". I have been humbled by the enormity of such a task yet incredibly honoured by the overwhelming gratitude* of the veterans. *The emphasis of this tribute is centred on their emotions: their compassion, their anxiety, their fatigue, and above all, their dedication.'*

I think one might have difficulty in justifying Glena Goodacre's sculpture as a fine work of art but it has found its place in the Vietnam Memorial complex as a matter of political expediency.

The memorials demonstrate how the government of a democratic society may respond to tragic events of this kind and, although America regretted the war, its military capability was not diminished.

Whilst in New York in 2001, I heard a New York taxi driver in a radio interview tell how he was always on the lookout for monuments. If he saw a new one he would ask his fare if he might switch the meter off, stop his cab and take a photo. I did try to track him down to no avail; a man after my own heart.

# ✧ Chapter Four ✧
# My Revolution

*Cawnpore Memorial*

There has never been a time in my adult life when I did not know where my passport was. The opportunity to travel the world only opened up with the arrival of cheap air fares in the 1960s. After returning from my holiday with Mervyn, working for the American firm Arthur Andersen, I soon started looking for another job. In those days, there were advertisements in newspapers under box numbers without a company name. I wrote enquiring and to my embarrassment, the firm in question were my employers Arthur Andersen and I was soon encouraged to move on. This turned out to be a good thing.

Between 1960 and retirement I worked for several firms. In 1962, I found a job working for the Scottish investment company William Baird & Co Ltd. Both the Sierra Leone Development Co and Clifford Williams were subsidiaries.

While working with Clifford Williams, who were then the largest trouser makers in Europe and supplier to Marks & Spencer, I often visited a trouser making factory in Northern Italy. The company won a contract to supply a million pairs of trousers to the Italian Army. Unfortunately, the prices were all incorrect. In Italy, the quotation should include all the trimmings, (i.e. buttons, zips, etc) but it transpired that the quote was without trimmings. Inevitably this investment was a not a success and eventually the company was sold.

However, my first job as a tax manager in 1965 was the most exciting, and perhaps the most fascinating and challenging, working with the Sierra Leone Development Company, known locally as DELCCO a British owned concern, which operated an iron ore mine in West Africa on a lease from the Government of Sierra Leone. As my father had studied tropical medicine there long before, there was an attraction in visiting the country where he had spent part of his career. Payment for the right to extract ore was made in the form of an income tax which was administered by the British Government.

Sierra Leone (meaning 'Lion Mountains' in Portuguese) had been part of the British

Empire for about two hundred years when it was established as a home for freed slaves. These people came mostly from plantations in Virginia in the American South. The British had promised them freedom if they fought on their side in the Revolutionary War. After the British were defeated, the former slaves naturally wanted their freedom, so the British transported many of them to Sierra Leone which was thought to have a similar climate to the American South.

Following Harold Macmillan's 'Wind of Change' speech in Cape Town in 1960 about the need to hand power over to the black population, the British colonial government began to withdraw from Africa and Sierra Leone was becoming an independent state. It was unacceptable to their national pride for the former colonial power to control their tax revenues. Also, the British Government wished to get rid of a troublesome and potentially contentious arrangement. I was charged with aiding this process.

On my first day in the office, I began to draft an agreement between the company and the Government which would take the form of an Act of Parliament in Sierra Leone. I wrote the words, 'Be it enacted by the Queen's Most

Excellent Majesty by and with the consent of the Parliament of Sierra Leone'. I found myself negotiating with the local dictator, who had taken over from the administration left behind by the British, and the Head of the Tax Department.

At this stage I felt Sierra Leone was a desperately poor and disease-ridden country with a hot climate. Its only resources were minerals and there were important diamond reserves but unfortunately protecting diamonds from theft was almost impossible. Iron ore reserves were very profitable during and after the Second World War which were supplied to munitions factories in England and to steel works in Europe.

Economics of Sierra Leone mining changed dramatically with the coming of big ore carriers which meant it was possible to bring in ore from Australia and South America more cheaply than production shipped directly to Europe. Sierra Leone's Development Company's harbour could only accommodate small ships which were uneconomic on long journeys.

When I went to work for the Company at its office in the City of London, I spent most of my time talking to mining engineers. I was trying to establish the economic realities behind the business, and which made money and which lost money. I found that the company was engaged in a major capital expenditure programme constructing a new pier and railway. It was important to get this expense put in the appropriate classification for tax purposes and to distinguish between the cost of buildings and the cost of plants and machinery. Plant and machinery could be written off at a hundred per cent, giving a considerable tax saving, whereas buildings were written off over ten or twenty years which is far less advantageous. I discovered, working through the records, that the classification had been incorrectly made. In most cases, we had machinery of all sorts on the mine. The machinery was covered by zinc cladding for protection from the rain. I asked the chief engineer if the machinery would work without cladding. He said, 'if it makes a difference to tax, I shall issue everyone raincoats and take the cladding away'. I put this point to the Revenue who said if this was correct they would concede a hundred per cent write-off.

The amounts involved were substantial, several million pounds, and I was rather pleased with myself. It never seemed to occur to the accountants that this was an obvious analysis which had been overlooked, but I said nothing about that.

However, at an early stage in my employment I found myself in trouble. Reading the agreement, I found that tax had been overpaid by DELCCO who were entitled to a substantial refund from the Sierra Leone government. However, the managing director, a red-faced Scotsman, stormed into my room and said, 'Do you know what you've done? I have just had lunch with the Minister of Finance who says if he has to repay the tax he won't be able to pay the police or the army and there will be a revolution and a civil war. Fix this.' We did but with great difficulty – by the company lending the government the money to enable them to pay us back the tax overpaid. Sadly, the economics of the mine became difficult and the investment was largely lost. This was a very sad event for me and for the workers concerned, particularly the poor Africans who were almost totally dependent on this uneconomic mine.

I was alarmed that in my innocence, I could have caused a revolution. It taught me a valuable lesson; always proceed with caution in foreign parts.

I went twice on negotiating trips to

Sierra Leone, the first time in 1965, flying from Gatwick to Madeira where we stayed overnight (very popular with mining personnel as excellent duty-free shop). We then flew on to Freetown and stayed in a hotel there for about a week. Roads in Sierra Leone were not good at this time but travelling round a tropical country in a Land Rover was a great experience for me.

Freetown still had some of the atmosphere of a British colony, complete with a war memorial designed by Edwin Lutyens found outside the Secretariat Building where our meetings took place. The memorial, organised by the War Graves Commission, commemorates local servicemen from Sierra Leone, one thousand, one hundred and nine lost in the First World War and two hundred and forty-seven in the Second World war.

On the last day of one of our trips to Sierra Leone, two British mining companies working there gave a party to which I was invited. Many people were there, some expatriates, some Sierra Leone business people and officials. It was fascinating to see how people mixed at this function. As the party came to an end, I was talking to the Chief Justice of Sierra Leone who asked me to visit his new Court House the next morning. This was a considerable honour but I was rather concerned about the protocol. In Africa, it is customary to make small gifts to people, called a dash in Sierra Leone. My boss said, as he disappeared laughing into the lift, he used to give the Chief Justices' predecessor about five pounds. I knew not to over tip. On the other hand, I did not fancy being on some charge being accused of bribing an official. It was the only time in my business career I had a sleepless night worrying about how much to tip. The next morning, I kept my appointment, the Chief Justice sent a message he was unable to accompany me and sent his police orderly. I was relieved as I thought there would be no harm in tipping the policeman who took me around the Court House who was as happy as a sergeant when I gave him five pounds. Since those days, Sierra Leone has been through horrible epidemics and a civil war with an almost a total collapse of its iron ore mining industry.

When I was a child, because of British rule, contact with India was very strong. Many British soldiers were sent to India in connection with the Japanese war. My school had Old Boys' Associations all over India for those from Britain who had gone to serve in India. The war memorial at Winchester College has plaques for the major provinces of British India, not because many Indians were Wykehamists (former pupils of Winchester College), but because so many Wykehamists and their fathers served in India. Now we see a reverse movement of people – many Indians have gone to English speaking countries of the world.

The Rohillas were a warrior tribe from Afghanistan that moved to Northern India in the late eighteenth century and with the help of the India East India Company, Faizullah Khan (1730-1794) was installed as ruler. After his death, his ill-tempered and over bearing sons began contending with each other for the throne. The Indian forces fought to eject them under the command of General Sir Robert Abercromby (1740-1827) and the casualties of the Second Rohilla War in 1794, are commemorated by two memorials.

In the grounds of St John's Church in Calcutta, the Rohilla monument, erected in 1817, is a domed cenotaph supported by twelve Doric columns with an elaborate classical freeze including shields and the skulls of oxen (bucrania). This fine neo-classical pavilion, over fifty feet high, is based on Sir

William Chambers' (1723-96) Temple at Kew. As a young man, Chambers spent nine years in India and China with the Swedish East India Company. At the foot is an inscription: *'To the Indian Officers and the European and native non-commissioned officers and privates who were killed in the second Rohilla War in India 1794.'*

A second memorial on the battlefield at Fatehaganj, near Bareilly, consists of a square-shaped tower about seven feet high on a platform fourteen feet by fourteen feet. The epitaph, with an inscription similar to the monument in Calcutta, reads: *'Erected by order of the Governor General in Council'*

The monument sadly, is now in a poor state of repair. It is surrounded by a wall, and over the gate is written: 'Christian Graveyard. The Free Will Baptist Church of India.' If this is in fact the site of the burial of the dead of the conflict, it is one of the earliest military cemeteries in modern times. Nearby there is an Indian graveyard with tombs of the Rohilla dead.

The Black Hole of Calcutta is also commemorated by a monument in the grounds of St John's Church. In 1756, the small British settlement in Calcutta was occupied by the Marathas, an Indian tribe. Overnight one hundred and forty-six English prisoners were crammed in the torrid heat of June, into a room eighteen feet square. Only twenty-three survivors emerged alive the next morning from what is known in British history as the Black Hole of Calcutta. The accuracy of these casualties is disputed by modern historians and the event is regarded as crude British propaganda by many Indians. Following the capture of Calcutta, Robert Clive travelled from Madras to reconquer the city and to establish British control of Bengal.

John Zephaniah Holwell a former prisoner, erected a tablet on the site of the 'Black Hole' to commemorate the victims but it disappeared at some point before 1822. When Lord Curzon (1859-1925) became Viceroy in 1899, he noticed that there was nothing to mark the spot and commissioned a new monument consisting of an octagonal obelisk situated near the Writers' Building (government offices). It was erected in 1901 at the corner of Dalhousie Square, said to be the site of the 'Black Hole'. This mentioned the prior existence of Holwell's tablet. During an anti-monument movement by the Indians in India 1940, it was removed from Dalhousie Square and re-erected in the graveyard of St

John's Church, where it remains.

Why Curzon chose to revive unhappy memories in this way is not clear. Curzon was keenly interested in the preservation of Indian buildings and devoted a great deal of energy and of his own money (or perhaps that of his two American heiress wives) for his projects. He was particularly interested in the restoration of the Taj Mahal. Jawaharlal Nehru (1889-1964), the first prime minister of Independent India, said in relation to Curzon's work with the Archaeological Survey of India, 'After every other Viceroy has been forgotten, Curzon will be remembered because he reinstated all that was beautiful in India.'

Major loss of life for the British took place in the Siege of Cawnpore in 1857, known as Kanpur today. The garrison was in an indefensible position and apparently exchanged surrender for a safe conduct to the Ganges where boats were to take the English soldiers, together with their wives and children, down river. However, as they were embarking at the river they were attacked and nearly all the men were killed by local people. Almost two hundred women and children were taken back to Cawnpore and confined in a small bungalow, and they were killed as the British relieving force approached. The Mutineers, the Indian soldiers, refused to kill them and they too were slaughtered by local butchers who threw their dismembered bodies into a well. The British troops were horrified at what they found and terrible vengeance was taken upon all those in Cawnpore. 'Remember Cawnpore' became the rallying cry for the British soldiers.

After peace had been restored, a memorial garden was built in the area of the well and a monument by Baron Marochetti (1805-1867) of a grieving angel, with eyes downcast, was placed over the well. Marochetti, although Italian, was a leading sculptor in Victorian England and was well known as Queen Victoria's favourite sculptor. The memorial park was surrounded by a pierced gothic screen designed by Sir Henry Yule (1820-1889), British Orientalist. The gateway has an inscription: *'These are they which come out of the great tribulation.'*

After Independence, the memorial garden was moved to a site near the memorial chapel. Here, Marochetti's angel made of white marble stands with eyes downcast. At the base of a rustic cross with arms crossed supporting, palms held upwards. The wings sweep down to the base at either side. The head is masterly, slightly inclined to one side with an expression which is at once stern and sorrowful.

The National Army Museum in London has a statue of Walter Hamilton VC (1856-1879) who died defending the British Mission in Kabul in Afghanistan. Hamilton, of the Regiment of Guides in the Indian Army, was an Irishman who had won a VC shortly before the incident at Kabul. He commanded a small force of Sikhs guarding the British Mission when it was attacked by the Afghans. Hamilton, his British officers, and his men were all killed or wounded. After all the British officers were dead, the Sikhs, although offered safe conduct, refused to surrender out of loyalty to the British Army. The Irish felt that Hamilton's monument was a symbol of British colonialism and it was removed from Dublin and allowed to decay. The statue was rescued and restored at great expense by the National Army Museum, when the Irish had the cheek to ask if they could have it back.

Indian Army Regimental memorials left behind by the British are still maintained in the traditional way and indeed the Indian Army and Air Force have their own memorials to the conflicts of the past ninety years.

A fine monument was erected at the Guides

Regimental Depot at Mardan in Pakistan, formerly part of India.

When I saw it many years ago, it was beautifully maintained by the Pakistan authorities. My wife and I met a very elderly guardian, or Chowkidar, who, when he realised we were from England, disappeared returning wearing a clean shirt with his medal ribbons from the 1939-45 war. I explained that I had a friend who had been born at Mardan where his father was Colonel of the Guides. The Chowkidar's eyes filled with tears, he came smartly to attention and said, 'Colonel Sahib'. I have never felt such a social failure in my life. It was all too difficult to explain that I was not a

*The Guides Memorial*

Colonel or anything else to do with the British Army. Much to my shame, I did not attempt to correct him. This was the only time I was ever called 'Sahib' in India. The expression has totally disappeared.

British visitors to this memorial are struck with the superb turn out of troops on parade and the extent to which almost eighty years after independence, the traditional style has apparently been maintained. I saw on television a group of men and women in what I thought was RAF uniform. I then realised they were flight crews for the Pakistan Air Force which had started to recruit women fighter pilots.

In 1857, part of the Indian Army mutinied soon after the Crimean War. The insurrection was soon effectively suppressed, perhaps because of what the British Army had learnt from their difficulties in the Crimea. Many memorials were erected in India including one on the Ridge at Delhi and at the Residency at Lucknow, which had been besieged, and was preserved as a ruin.

Lucknow was an important centre of British resistance to the rising. Lucknow, was the capital of the State of Oudh, which had recently been annexed by the British. Anticipating insurrection, the British Commander, Sir

Henry Lawrence, fortified and provisioned the British Residency which had been built in the 1780s. Although described as the Siege of Lucknow, in fact it was a siege of the Residency at Lucknow. In May 1857, the native regiments in Lucknow broke into a frenzy of looting and killing. After an unsuccessful attempt by British troops to defeat the mutineers, the siege began. Seventeen hundred troops, nearly half of them loyal sepoys, held the Residency against sixty thousand rebels. In Oudh, unlike most of India, the general population joined the rebels. In September, reinforcements led by Sir Henry Havelock, fought their way in but were unable to stop the siege. After a further British attack in November it was possible to evacuate the garrison but the Residency was not restored to British control until the spring of 1858. The Residency was almost completely destroyed in the siege. Women and children had been able to survive in the cellars which offered some protection from the heat in hot weather. The casualties were severe. Two thousand men, women and children were killed or died in the course of the siege.

The distinguishing feature of the Residency had been an octagonal corner staircase, crowned by a shallow cupola. From this tower, the Union

Flag was flown day and night, throughout the siege. The flag continued to fly day and night after the siege, the only place in the British Empire where the flag was not lowered at sunset until 1947 when the British withdrew from India. In great secrecy, the British personnel, led by a Major General of the Royal Engineers, removed the flag and flagstaff, and cemented in the base to prevent a premature rising of the new flag of Independent India, anticipating a triumphalist demonstration by Indian nationals. The Union Flag was delivered to King George VI at Windsor Castle where it was placed in the Royal Library Museum.

The ruins were preserved as an icon of British India and were laid out with lawns and flowerbeds. There are many memorials to those who perished in the siege. On the lawn in front of the Residency is a marble runic cross inscribed:

*'In memory of*
*Major-General Sir Henry Lawrence*
*K.C.B.*
*And the brave men who fell*
*In defence of the Residency*
*1857.'*

In the cemetery, there is a tomb for Sir Henry Lawrence with his own epitaph:

*'Here lies*

*The Residency, Lucknow*

Henry Lawrence
*Who tried to do his duty.*
*May the Lord have mercy on his soul.*
*Born 28th of June 1806*
*Died 4th of July 1857.'*

Although the graves appear to be intact, many graves were opened after the British withdrew in November 1857 in a search for treasure which might have been buried with the dead. After the British resumed control, the remains of the dead were re-buried in great secrecy to avoid further distress to their relatives. Many plaques refer to the gallantry of the defenders, including one to the devotion, gallantry and fidelity of the native officers and sepoys.

In fact, with great generosity, British

memorials have been reasonably maintained since Independence. There are relatively few memorials in this country to the fighting in India in 1857. Perhaps the war was less popular than the Crimea because it was further away and less well reported, or perhaps the British public were unhappy about the cruelty with which the mutiny was suppressed. Apart from the Westminster School memorial, I am not aware of a major public monument in London to the fighting of 1857.

Nearby is La Martinière Boys School, formerly Constantina. This is a remarkable building, designed by Major-General Claude Martin (*1735-1800*), a French Soldier of Fortune from Lyons, who came to India with the French East India Company. When the French were forced to leave India, Martin changed sides and worked with the British. He was a man of many parts and left his fortune to found schools in Lucknow, Calcutta and in his home town, Lyons, and these schools still survive.

Anticipating an attempt to seize his house by a local ruler after he died, he had the foresight to arrange to be buried in the basement which would make it unclean for Muslims to live there. La Martinière was almost certainly the school Rudyard Kipling's Kim attended and was the leading school for the education of British boys in India in the nineteenth century. In the Mutiny pupils performed sterling service as the Martinière Contingent. The headmaster, as well as a number of boys, were killed. La Martinière became the only school in the world to be awarded a ceremonial flag by the British Army, which is commonly referred to as the Battle Honours for the Defence of Lucknow 1857.

One memorial to a Victorian hero is that to Captain William Peel VC (1824-1858) and the crew of HMS Shannon. Peel, son of the Prime Minister Robert Peel, was awarded the VC in the Navy in the Crimean War. Later, Peel was taking his ship to the China Station when news came of trouble in India and he sailed to Calcutta. There he off-loaded a large naval gun from the Shannon to be transported up-river as far as possible, and then hauled over land to Lucknow. The British community in Calcutta greeted Peel enthusiastically and the Anglican Bishop, eighty-four years old, said that 'If he were a younger man, he would go with Peel's sailors.' Peel was wounded and died of fever on the journey, but the gun reached Lucknow where it was used in raising the siege. Until some years ago, the remains of the gun were in the ruins of the Residence. A statue of Peel has been preserved in a Government Sculpture Park near Calcutta. Originally Peel's statue was in a central position in the City. There have been rumours that the Indian authorities would allow the statue to be returned. However, it seems improbable the Indians would tolerate the reinstatement of a statue of a British hero of the Mutiny. There is also a memorial to Peel and the Shannon in Portsmouth. My wife and I saw the remains of what we were told were one of Peel's guns, when we visited the ruins of the Residency at Lucknow, many years ago.

I have visited Iran four times, twice before the fall of the Shah and twice afterwards. I first went to Iran on holiday in 1964 to stay with my aunts Amernouhie (Nouhie) and Emily who were formidable and adventurous women.

*Michael's Aunts Nouhie and Emily*

I returned via Israel and stayed at St George's Hostel in Jerusalem where I met Janet Lawrenson who was working for the Foreign Office in Israel. Janet stayed on in Israel for about three years and we married in August 1967 after she returned to the UK.

I am interested in the history of their war memorials and on my second visit, I found some distinguished cemeteries for the military dead in Isfahan and Tehran.

*The Rose Garden of the Martyrs, Isfahan*

Isfahan, now a UNESCO-designated World Heritage site, has the Rose Garden for Martyrs, a cemetery where at least seven thousand young volunteers killed during the Iran-Iraq war (1990-98) are buried. After hostilities ended, in a gesture of good will, the dead from both sides were exchanged and burial arrangements were reported in newspapers.

A photograph of the deceased marks each tomb in a simple white frame. On the back of each is another photograph, that of the Ayatollah Khomeini (1902-89) Head of State and religious leader during the war. The Isfahan cemeteries are well maintained and carefully follow teachings of Islam.

In Tehran, there are museums commemorating the dead and their losses. At the Holy Defence Museum, the 'Hall of Butterflies' is the name given to the memorial to the soldiers who died during the Iran-Iraq war. Display cases show personal memorabilia found on the fallen.

My aunt Nouhie adopted two Iranian children; Gohad Taj and Yadulla. Their father was almost one hundred years old when he asked Nouhie to take care of them. Their mother was a young servant girl and, given his advanced age, he wished to give them a better future. The children were sent off to school to get a good education. After leaving school, Yadulla was sent to the nurses' training school as British Petroleum had a hospital for their staff in Abadan.

Gohad Taj became a Petroleum engineer.

My wife and I saw them about thirty years ago, they took us to the Oil Company Senior Staff club in Tehran. Unfortunately, we lost touch and with all the wars in Iran, I do not know what happened to them but think they went to California. I am going to make enquiries about their fate.

My Aunt Emily was head of the Behesht-Ayin School in Isfahan (previously the Stileman Memorial School) where Queen Soraya (*1932-2001*) had been a pupil. My family fable is that my aunt was asked to suggest a bride for the Shah after the collapse of his first marriage. After Soraya's divorce, I was told my aunt was approached to suggest another suitable bride, but declined. I wonder if there is any truth in the story. Long ago, I believe Soraya mentioned my aunt in her autobiography, but my memory may be at fault.

After she had to leave her government school because of political pressure, Aunt Emily became Head of the Armenian Girls High School in Julfa. My other Aunt Nouhie worked in schools in Yezd and Isfahan and eventually she retired and went to live in the old Church Missionary Society Blind School where she died in her nineties.

*Aunt Nouhie meeting the Queen Mother*

When the Queen Mother went to Iran in April 1975 and visited Isfahan, a reception was held for her in the old British consulate building which had been handed over to the British Council. My Aunt Nouhie was confined to a wheelchair as she had broken her leg in a fall and was sitting out in the garden as she was unable to go to the party. The Queen Mother asked who the old lady was. She was told and she walked across the courtyard to greet her to the horror of the police who were concerned there would be an international incident. Life in Iran was never dull.

My aunts knew Sir Arnold Wilson (1884-1940), a British soldier turned politician, who mentions having a meal with missionaries in

Isfahan in his book called 'South West Persia' published in 1940. Wilson's adventures in Persia are described in his diary and letters home. My Aunt Emily carried despatches for him in Iran during the First World War with an escort of Indian Lancers.

Sir Arnold Wilson, full of late Victorian ideas of duty, patriotism and simple Christianity was educated at Clifton. He was the son of the headmaster of Clifton which is perhaps why I was sent there. He went to Sandhurst (passed out First) and joined the Indian Army. As a young officer, he was sent to Persia to command a group of Indian soldiers protecting the original British Petroleum drilling team at Ahwaz. Wilson was present when oil was first discovered in 1908. He scooped the oil company news by a month by sending a reference to the Psalms as a message in code to the Foreign Office which said, 'See Psalm 104 verse 15' (That he may bring (food) out of the earth ... and oil to make him a cheerful countenance).

Wilson remained in Iran until 1914 working in the political service of the Government of India, wore native clothes, was attacked three times by tribesmen, captured twice and succeeded in escaping. While in

Persia he was constantly studying British and Persian history and English Literature from a succession of books sent to him by his parents and borrowed locally. He wrote many volumes of official reports for the Government of India. In 1914, he was in charge of administration for the joint British/Persian/Turkish/Russian team demarcating the frontier between the Persian and Turkish Empires from the Gulf to Ararat. Wilson narrowly escaped internment by the Turks on the outbreak of war in 1914.

In the 1914-18 war Wilson served in Mesopotamia and was awarded the DSO on active service and received six mentions in Despatches. Eventually he became civil administrator in Baghdad with important responsibilities throughout the territory which eventually became Iraq. Wilson tried to establish Iraq as a British protectorate. This policy was not acceptable either to the fiercely nationalistic local population or to the war weary government at home. In 1921, he joined the company which eventually became British Petroleum and worked for it in Persia and London until 1932. In 1933, he became an independent member of parliament. Wilson was interested in social questions, health and welfare but his main concern lay in avoiding a European war (he had lost two brothers in the 1914-18 War) and to establish peace with Germany. He was also attracted to the discipline and approach of the Nazi party. Wilson became editor of the *Nineteenth Century and After*, a political publication. Wilson published several books of political and personal reminiscences and wrote several books about Persia and an apologia for his work in Iraq. Wilson also organised the great exhibition of Persian art in London in 1931.

In 1939, although well over military age, he joined the RAF as air crew. In May 1940, he spoke with great effect in the parliamentary debate which led to the collapse of the Chamberlain government and to Churchill's appointment as prime minister. Later that month Wilson was killed in action as a rear gunner. An up to date biography of this remarkable man is overdue.

Canada was originally settled by the French who explored far into the interior behind the Alleganies and down the great Mississippi river system into the Gulf of Mexico. The British conquered Canada at the Battle of Quebec 1759. General James Wolfe (*1727-1759*) was undoubtedly the greatest hero of the British community in Canada during the eighteenth century and one of Westminster Abbey's most ornate and romantic memorials was erected in 1772 to him. Joseph Wilton's sculpture shows the hero dying at the moment of victory at the Battle of Quebec. In classic allegorical style, Wolfe is shown naked, with his uniform at his feet, about to be crowned with a laurel wreath held by a symbolic Victory offering a palm.

The inscription reads:

*'TO THE MEMORY OF JAMES WOLFE*
*MAJOR-GENERAL AND COMMANDER*
*IN CHIEF OF THE BRITISH LAND*
*FORCES ON THE EXPEDITION*
*AGAINST QUEBEC WHO AFTER*
*SURMOUNTING BY ABILITY AND*
*VALOUR ALL OBSTACLES OF ART*
*AND NATURE WAS SLAIN IN THE*
*MOMENT OF VICTORY ON THE XIII OF*
*SEPTEMBER MDCCLIX. THE KING AND*
*THE PARLIAMENT OF GREAT BRITAIN*
*DEDICATE THIS MONUMENT.'*

This statue was inspired by Benjamin West's highly romanticised picture of the death of Wolfe, which itself derives from the traditional depiction of Christ's Deposition from the Cross. West painted several versions and one painted for King George III can be seen at Spencer House; another version is in Ottawa.

In 1759 Wolfe sailed up the St Lawrence River and, with his army, climbed the steep path to the Plains of Abraham (an area named for the farmer who owned the land). The French had withdrawn their troops from the Plains of Abraham because they did not believe the British could move an army up the narrow path. Wolfe defeated the French garrison, securing the key fortress of Canada, and thus North America, for Britain. Wolfe, receiving early wounds in the wrist and belly, was fatally wounded after being struck in the body and Louis-Joseph de Montcalm, the French Commander, was also wounded and died the next day. Quebec surrendered on September 18th, 1759. Wolfe's body was returned to England and was buried in the family vault at Greenwich.

Wolfe was not only a highly efficient soldier, but also a considerable romantic. As he was being rowed up the St. Lawrence towards the battle site, he recited to his officers from Gray's Elegy 'The Paths of Glory Lead but to the Grave', and said he would rather have written this poem than conquer Canada.

The most remarkable Canadian memorial is to be found at Vimy Ridge in France. The monument commemorates the successful attack by Canadian troops against the German army in 1917. It is also a memorial to the sixty thousand Canadians who died in France and, in my view, is perhaps the most distinguished single memorial in all of France. It was designed by Toronto architect Walter Allward (*1876-1955*) and consists of two tall obelisk-shaped pillars from which emerge a series of symbolic figures including Peace, Justice, Truth and Knowledge. The pillars are mounted on a massive base also containing sculpted figures notably Canada mourning her dead. A very impressive memorial when viewed from a distance but, close to, the detail of the sculpture intended to be seen from a distance, is less precise. Personally, I think it is not large enough to stand out from the valley floor below. One wonders if Allward saw the site before designing the memorial. The monument took eleven years to construct and was unveiled by King Edward VIII on 26th July 1936.

# ✧ Chapter Five ✧
# An Ear to the Ground

*The Grieving Parents*

In 1965, foreseeing a difficult future with DELCCO Sierra Leone Development Company, I persuaded my employers that I really wanted to work in the oil industry having been headhunted for Thomson by a retired colonel who served on the Montgomery staff during the war. Fortunately, my employers recognised that keeping me under pressure to work out my notice would not make for an efficient employee. Eventually the financial directors agreed to do a salary deal for me in that both sides would share my salary. This enabled me to move jobs but had the great disadvantage that I was to do two jobs at the same time.

Prior to joining Thomson officially, I wanted to see what was happening in the North Sea to see if I felt I could cope. Thomson people were a bit surprised at this as none of their accountants had been interested before in going to site. It was arranged that two accountants and the chief oil executive who had worked for Shell for many years and was an old hand, would accompany me on a trip to the North Sea. We flew to Aberdeen and travelled by helicopter along the coast of Scotland which was either green and pleasant looking or rocky and austere. The inside of the helicopter was about the same size as a mini. We followed the coast until we reached the drilling platform. I found this rather scary and was trying to will the pilot to follow the green bits, but it was mainly rocks. I was told that if we ditched we would die from the cold of the sea before we could be fished out. I insisted on having life insurance, at some expense to Thomson, just in case. Anyway, I was enormously impressed with the new structure which was being built and felt this was going to be a new chapter in British history, and indeed it was.

Soon adequate reserves of oil were found to support the development and the project went ahead. The Thomson financial arrangement was on a limited recourse basis, i.e. if the investment failed, the banks would lose money but Thomson borrowed nothing. This was an innovative arrangement in the UK.

I was a 'dirty boots accountant'. Always going to site to obtain information not otherwise available where we had responsibility to ensure compliance with tax law. What were the economics behind the business and how would profits be achieved? I felt financial people should be aware of the context in which their work would be seen and the need to maintain good relationships with governments and other companies in the industry.

Oil was something new to the UK government and part of the problem was the ignorance of the civil servants working for the government on the reality of life in the North Sea. Soon after joining Thomson in 1966, I proposed taking officials from the Inland Revenue who would be dealing with oil taxation to visit an oil rig in Scotland, with Oswald Davis, Head of the Tax Office for the oil industry, accompanied by financial and technical staff from the consortium. We flew up to Aberdeen where we boarded a helicopter to visit a drilling rig and a production platform. Being unsteady on my legs because of polio and afraid of heights it was quite an experience.

People were always puzzled that I travelled so much but I found this was the best way to find out what was going on. My employers, who knew that I had my ear to the ground, tolerated a great deal of travel. I think the senior people in the Thomson Company at the time of its rapid development were always in the air or on the road and with Concorde it was so easy.

My family and I had the opportunity to visit countries throughout the world. The cost of a first-class ticket to the United States the company would buy me enabled my family to travel economy class to California. I visited Canada many times, Japan, Hong Kong and China on business and visited around forty-five states, out of fifty, in the United States.

Concorde came into service about the same time as the Piper Oil field came into production. A great sense of relief descended on the office as we realised our plans were coming into fruition. The acquisition programme for businesses in the United States swung into action. Frequent travel to America was inevitable. The company view was that company executives were allowed to charge for business class fares to relieve travel fatigue and save time. The wife of a colleague in New York employed a travel agent able to arrange flights on Concorde for about the same cost as conventional business class fares.

Concorde did the transatlantic journey in about three and half hours rather than seven or eight hours on a conventional aircraft. The cabin was cramped, and it was desirable to sit near the front as the rear of the fuselage became very hot in flight. A great advantage was that there were no flights at night. I hated travelling overnight and not getting a proper rest.

One occasionally saw celebrities on these flights. One day former Prime Minister Ted Heath (*1916-2005*) was sitting behind me. I had read that he had been in New York writing criticism on a concert at Carnegie Hall. He settled down with the BA flight magazine and read nothing else on the entire flight. How he stretched this reading out I will never know.

I probably went on several hundred Concorde flights and only had one fright. Janet and I were travelling to England when halfway down the runway, at Kennedy Airport in New York our plane came to a grinding halt. The pilot made a consciously casual announcement that we needed a replacement part and would be delayed by half an hour to an hour. We landed in London an hour late. I had arranged a dinner meeting between Thomson's lawyer

David Wootton, subsequently Lord Mayor of London, from solicitors Allen & Overy and our accountants Price Waterhouse, to discuss a price sensitive transaction. We had booked a suite and ordered dinner at the Savoy.

After collapsing into bed after a successful meeting and going over our journey, my wife and I found we were in delayed shock by the Concorde experience. We realised had the breakdown occurred at the end of the runway instead of at the beginning, we would have ended up as strawberry jam.

Thomson owned Britannia Airways and the Chief Engineer said Concorde would fall to pieces in twelve months, in fact it ran for twenty years.

The chief executive once said to me the nicest thing I ever heard at work. 'With you around, whatever else I have to worry about, I never worry about tax.' I felt my job was to enable people to get on with running the business and making money and not for them to worry about tax.

After I joined Thomson my life became much more interesting. Exciting people were around, endless good gossip and great events happening. I was taken on a tour of *The Times* to see the paper being 'put to bed', i.e. printed and published. *The Times* was a difficult place to work because of the complex and difficult union relations. On one occasion Lord Thomson, then in his seventies, arrived in a taxi at the Gray's Inn Road after an overnight flight from Canada. Lord Thomson asked the porter to take his luggage upstairs and he replied, 'Sorry, sir, against union rules.' Not long after, the head office moved from the Gray's Inn Road to new premises.

One day I was sent for to attend a meeting with Michael Brown, financial director who had appointed me, and William Rees-Mogg, then editor of The Times. I was excited that perhaps my literary talents had been spotted and they were going to suggest a little tax column for the paper – no such luck. It had become apparent Bernard Levin (1928-2004), who was a leading journalist on *The Times* with a great following, was employed as freelance and was not covered by the company pension scheme. Indeed, he had made no provision for his old age at all. If the arrangement was changed there was a risk of a major industrial dispute as everyone else would want similar treatment.

I was sent off to talk to S.G. Warburg the investment bank where I saw Hugh Stevenson, a banker I had known when he worked as a trainee solicitor at Linklater & Paines when he helped with a difficulty at the Sierra Leone Development Company. Hugh produced an expert on pensions from the City who was able to restructure Levin's pension scheme without having to make disclosure in the accounts. (I totally forget how this was done.)

Anyway, sorting out Levin's pension scheme was a considerable little achievement for me and helped my standing in the company. From my point of view there was great entertainment value in meeting Bernard Levin and his advisors who had to be satisfied that the arrangement was valid and protected. I never knew what happened after Thomson sold *The Times* but I assume that Rupert Murdoch kept the arrangement as Levin continued to write on the paper. Encountering this brilliantly clever journalist was one of the more exciting moments of my work with *The Times*.

Another person of great interest in our little world was Anthony Armstrong Jones (*1930-2017*), Lord Snowdon, Princess Margaret's husband. Before I joined Thomson, the Snowdons would come to the Christmas lunch held in a city livery hall. Sadly, by the time I actually went, they were not having a happy relationship and neither came to the lunch. This was sad because I thought it was going to be the social pinnacle of my life. This was all a very exciting little world and made bearable the tedium of the extractive industry.

On another occasion, I was told the auditors were worrying about another problem related to Marmaduke Hussey (Duke) (1923-2006) who was general manager at *The Times* newspapers. Duke had been badly injured during the war and walked with difficulty and had to use a car all the time. The Company provided him with a car and driver twenty-four hours a day so that he could follow up on stories at very short notice any time. The auditors were saying this was a very substantial benefit in kind on which Duke could become personally liable to tax. If this had happened this would have been a substantial liability to the employer and the employee.

I thought I had better go and see Duke. I asked for an appointment to discuss a personal matter. I went around to see him at The Times. At the same moment that I arrived, who should turn up but Lord Snowdon carrying, I guess, cameras in a canvas bag such as plumbers used to use for their tools. I thought this was a rather clever idea because it would not be apparent that he was carrying valuables.

Anyway, in the porter's room in the Gray's Inn Road, we arrived together. I was waving to encourage Lord Snowdon to go ahead as I could not remember why I was there, what I was doing or what I was going to say. I followed and went up to see Duke who said aggressively, 'I understand this is a personal matter; personal to you or personal to me?' I suppose he was expecting me to complain about the way I had been treated by somebody. I then explained the difficulty and he said we would have to find a solution to this one. I did not think it was very serious, only a nuisance.

We then had a nice gossip about how he had been shot by a Prussian guard in Finland during the war. The Finns were allies of the Germans in the Second World War.

What I did not know at this time was that Duke's wife was Lady Susan Hussey who was the Queen's principal lady-in-waiting at the time and accompanied her on all of her important visits. Had I known this it would have been very useful information because I think no sane inspector of taxes would be applying a rather absurd tax charge to a national hero whose wife was a close friend of the Queen.

✳ ✳ ✳

Some years ago, Janet and I paid a visit to Greece looking at ancient monuments. Thompson Travel arranged for a car and guide and we visited the principal sites. We were particularly interested because of the wars with Iran.

Whilst visiting Marathon and Thermopylae, we went to the nearby hot springs, which according to mythology were created by the god Hephaestus as a gift for Hercules. When we arrived, we found a lorry driver had parked, stripped off and was shaving in one of the springs.

War memorials began with the ancient Greeks about two thousand five hundred years ago. The earliest memorials commemorated the Greeks who lost their lives defending their country against the Persian invasions. Athens like other Greek states in ancient times was a democracy which needed to persuade its young men to fight, its women and old people to accept the sacrifice of the lives of their husbands, sons and lovers. There were two major invasions. In 490 BC, a huge Persian army attacked the Greeks and was defeated on the shore at Marathon. The Athenians won a stunning victory with one hundred and eighty-seven dead and many thousands of Persians killed. The news was sent by a messenger to

Athens who, after running the twenty-nine miles from the battle to the city, said 'victory' and dropped dead.

The Parthenon in Athens was built as a memorial to the Athenians who lost their lives at the Battle of Marathon. The famous frieze from the temple, now mostly in the British Museum, London, contained one hundred and eighty-six statues, traditionally the number of the Athenian dead at Marathon so this is arguably a war memorial in itself, as indeed is the marathon race held all over the world to commemorate the runner. I wonder how many of those taking place realise they are involved in a kind of war memorial. A reproduction of the frieze is displayed on the walls at Holborn underground station and is passed daily without notice by thousands of London commuters.

*The Parthenon*

Normally the bodies of the Athenians were cremated on the field of battle and their ashes taken to Athens for ceremonial burial in a public cemetery, with speeches from civil leaders. After Marathon, as a mark of special honour, the Athenians were buried at a site near the battlefield. A monument built on the site has long since disappeared but the mound can still be seen.

Later a great temple to the goddess Athena was built in Athens on the Acropolis with one hundred and eighty-seven statues. An Oxford archaeologist, Sir John Boardman (*1927–*), has a theory that, as this is the same number as Athenian dead in the battle, it was therefore a monument to the war dead.

Ten years after their repulse at Marathon the Persians attacked Greece again. Another huge army marched from Asia crossing the Hellespont (a narrow natural strait now known as Dardanelles) on a bridge of boats and encountered a small Spartan force of three hundred men at Thermopylae on the coast. The Spartans, until they were all killed or wounded, held up the Persian Army.

A monument was erected with the inscription:

*'Go tell the Spartans thou that passeth by,*
*That here obedient to their laws we lie.'*

This monument stood for nearly a thousand years and was described by travellers in Roman times, and the phrase has been repeated in the past two hundred years on many modern war memorials demonstrating the influence of Greek revival on modern thought. One can still see the little hill on which the Spartan King Leonidas made his last stand.

My missionary aunt Emily teaching in Iran, acquired an assistant Mary Isaac. Mary was on her way to China when civil war broke out there so she was diverted to Iran where she then worked and lived for many years. Teaching a class of demure Iranian girls, she said that the Greeks won the war against Persia at Thermopylae. The class all yelled out 'No they didn't'. Mary was a bit embarrassed by this and looked up the history afterwards and found that in fact the Persians did win that war although the Greeks put up a stalwart resistance whilst vastly outnumbered. The Spartan resistance was not a futile gesture, but gave the Greeks time to organise their defence and to assemble their forces which eventually defeated the Persians at the Battle of Platea.

I once gave a talk to the National Army Museum about war memorials with the title

'Go Tell the Spartans'. In my innocence, I assumed that everyone would know about this epic battle but, after my talk, I was approached by a nice old boy with a fine military moustache who said to me 'I never knew we had a war with the Spartans'. I did not attempt to explain.

In Ireland, I set up a joint venture between Thomson and the *Irish Times* for a computer based financial information system. I was also involved with the *Belfast Telegraph* which was a successful Thomson newspaper which still exists.

The finest Nelson monument was his column in Dublin. The IRA thought this a symbol of British supremacy and had it destroyed. The IRA sub-contracted the job to a French demolition expert who did a neat job, blowing up the column without any other damage. The Irish government then told the Irish army to finish the column off and to destroy its base. The army did so and blew out all the windows in O'Connell Street. My father, who had been brought up in Dublin, said that Éamon De Valera (*1882-1975*), one of the dominant political figures in twentieth century Ireland and a leader in the struggle for independence, asked that the site be kept. There was a question whether the Pillar was a memorial to a casualty in war, Admiral Nelson, killed at the Battle of Trafalgar 1805, or a symbol of British Power in Ireland.

The memorial to the Irish Brigade in Gettysburg by William Rudolph O'Donovan (*1844-1920*), erected in 1880, is in the form of a Celtic Cross with an Irish Wolfhound lying at the foot of the cross, a symbol of canine courage, strength and fidelity. In the British and American armies, Irish Wolfhounds are regimental mascots. Christian symbolism is unusual on American war memorials but

common in the British Isles. The Celtic cross is often used in Ireland.

Driven from Ireland by the desperate poverty which followed the great famine in the 1840s, many young Irishmen enlisted

*Memorial to the Irish Brigade* in the Union and

Confederate Armies, often as substitutes for draftees. Rich Americans hired substitutes, thus reducing the impact on the moneyed classes of the heavy casualties in the war. In Britain in the First World War, casualties among the aristocracy and upper classes were not proportionate to their numbers, perhaps due to the public-school system which encouraged military service. This was not the case in America where the rich could buy substitutes for the draft. President Theodore Roosevelt was embarrassed because his father, married to a southerner, sent a substitute and did not take part in the war.

The memorial to the 116th Pennsylvania Infantry, a part of the Irish Brigade, has on its side a shamrock, symbol of Ireland, with a platform on which a fallen soldier is depicted lying on the field. Major St Claire Mulholland commanding the 116th Regiment went forward during a lull in the fighting to the spot where the 110th Pennsylvanian had been engaged earlier in the day. He was awed by the sight of a young soldier, shot through the head, with a faint smile visible on his face. The memory of this scene was the inspiration for the monument, which is unusual in the English-speaking world but less so in France, in depicting death on the field of battle. This is an unusual presentation for the period, but becomes more common in the late twentieth century due to media photographs and television during the Vietnam War, when for many people, the horrors of war became better known.

*Father Corby, Chaplain in the Irish Brigade*

A statue of Father William Corby, chaplain to a regiment in the Irish Brigade, was erected by Samuel Murray, and shows him standing on a boulder before the troops marched off to battle, calling upon God to grant them courage, and pronounced Absolution should they die. Later Father Corby became President of the Catholic University of Notre Dame, where my son-in-law was educated.

\* \* \*

I visited Switzerland three or four times a year as Thomson had a finance and leasing company with an office in Zug. This enabled me to visit one of my favourite memorials, The Dying Lion of Lucerne.

*Dying Lion of Lucerne*

Visitors to such a staunchly neutral country as Switzerland may be surprised to find one of the finest war memorials in Europe. On a summer's day in Lucerne one can witness coach upon coach of loyal citizens of the Swiss Confederation come to admire their dying lion, looking languidly out across the turquoise lake.

Renaissance Switzerland was an impoverished place with few natural resources. Soldiering was an unexpected remedy for this – the Swiss sold their services as mercenary soldiers in countless Italian conflicts, on both sides, and in the eighteenth century, Swiss mercenaries served with the British and the French armies in their wars in India.

From the seventeenth century onwards, the King of France had a bodyguard composed of Swiss soldiers.

Today the only Swiss mercenaries are in the service of the Pope providing the Papal Guard at the Vatican. Michelangelo is sometimes given credit for their beautifully distinctive uniforms. The vibrant blue, yellow and red–the colours of the Medici–have been used since the 1600s, with only minor changes through the centuries. In fact, it was Commandant Jules Repond who designed the modern uniforms in 1914, drawing inspiration from Raphael's frescoes.

During the French Revolution, when the mob broke in to the Tuileries Palace the Swiss guards tried to eject them, but King Louis XVI issued orders that the Swiss were to return to their barracks and not to fight. However, this only happened after their position could not be held. Eventually most were killed or wounded, passively taking their blows and flesh-wounds in accordance with the King's orders. The King and his family left by a side entrance.

In 1818, once Switzerland had regained its independence after the defeat of Napoleon, an officer of the guards, who had been on leave in Lucerne at the time of the attack on the Tuileries, began to collect money for a monument.

The Danish sculptor Bertel Thorvaldsen (*1770-1884*) was commissioned to design the memorial – a dying lion impaled on a spear. A Swiss craftsman, Lucas Ahorn (*1789-1856*), carved it into the rock face of Lake Lucerne.

The monument measures ten metres in length and six metres in height and is dedicated to the *Fidei ac Virtuti*, the loyalty and bravery of the Swiss. The lion covers a shield bearing the fleur-de-lis of the French monarchy. Beside the lion is another shield bearing the arms of Switzerland. The inscription below the sculpture lists the names of the officers who lost their lives and the approximate numbers of soldiers of those who died (seven hundred and sixty) and who survived (three hundred and fifty).

Mark Twain captures the scene with

touching elegance in his book 'A Tramp Abroad' 1880.

*'The Lion lies in his lair in the perpendicular face of a low cliff – for he is carved from the living rock of the cliff. His size is colossal, his attitude is noble. His head is bowed, the broken spear is sticking in his shoulder, his protecting paw rests upon the lilies of France. Vines hang down the cliff and wave in the wind, and a clear stream trickles from above and empties into a pond at the base, and in the smooth surface of the pond the lion is mirrored among the water-lilies.*

*Around about are green trees and grass. The place is a sheltered, reposeful woodland nook, remote from noise and stir and confusion – and all this is fitting, for lions do die in such places, and not on granite pedestals in public squares fenced with fancy iron railings. The Lion of Lucerne would be impressive anywhere, but nowhere so impressive as where he is.'*

In most countries attitudes to war and changes in public opinion can be traced from memorials to the war dead. The vicissitudes of the history of Russia and changing interpretations of that history mean that attitudes to the war reflected in war memorials vary from time to time. For example, Russia is almost the only European country with no memorials to the dead of the First World War which the Bolshevik Revolutionaries felt was an imperialist conflict best forgotten. In 1918, the Russian Imperial family was killed by the Bolsheviks and every effort was made to destroy their remains.

After the collapse of the Soviet Union the bodies of the Imperial family were re-buried in the Orthodox Cathedral in St Petersburg and the family canonised. The authenticity of the remains has been established by DNA evidence provided by the Queen's husband the Duke of Edinburgh who has a direct relationship through his mother to the Imperial Family. In a sense, their graves are now memorials to victims of war.

In 1812, the French invasion was initially successful. Moscow was occupied after the inconclusive Battle of Borodino, but the absence of supplies in the cold Russian winter meant the French army had to retire, suffering heavy casualties in the retreat. Napoleon's Imperial Army returned to Poland with only a shadow of the force which had entered Russia. After the fall of Napoleon, the Russian army marched across Europe and occupied Paris.

In contrast, many memorials were erected to casualties in the Great Patriotic War

(*1941-45*) as it is called in Russia, both within the Soviet Union and in the conquered territories of Eastern Europe. In 1941, Hitler reached the outskirts of Moscow but failed to capture the city and the German army eventually was defeated by the Russian armies. Russia ended the Second World War as a major economic and military power as happened after the defeat of Napoleon's invasion.

The Russian people united almost spontaneously to defeat the invasions of 1812 and 1941. The Second World War is known in Russia as the Great Patriotic War. This is not an unjust title because the whole people united to defeat the invaders notwithstanding their sufferings under communism and accepted terrible privations in defence of their country. The well-known sufferings, including cannibalism, of the besieged people of Leningrad were terrible but probably no worse than those of civilians elsewhere in Russia. After 1812, churches and cathedrals were erected as offerings to Divine Providence for assisting in the defeat of the French invaders, but not to the memory of the soldiers who lost their lives. The force of Russian patriotism and nationalism should not be underestimated.

The Crimean War, fought from 1853

to 1856, was one of the first modern wars in which the sacrifices of the military dead were memorialised. The war in the Crimea was the first conflict in which the combatants of both sides sought to give their men proper burial. The Russians began by burying their officers in marked graves either in cemeteries on the battlefield or in towns close to military hospitals where many men on both sides died, either from wounds or from disease. Funerals of a somewhat perfunctory nature were conducted by chaplains accompanying the troops.

During the course of the war the British laid out cemeteries for their dead on the battlefield. Tombstones, particularly for officers, were erected on the battlefield or in cemeteries. Commemorative stones for different regiments were also erected with memorials for non-commissioned officers and other ranks. These were placed close to where the men had died. Many thousands of men died in hospital or were buried in mass graves adjacent to the hospitals.

The Crimean War was accepted in Britain, fought, it was felt by the public, to prevent the Russians from taking control of the holy places in Palestine and to protect the British Empire in India and the East from Russian control of the Eastern Mediterranean. The war was followed by the erection of memorials in many places for the soldiers who lost their lives in terrible conditions.

The Crimean war is regarded as a shameful national defeat by Russia in contrast with the ignominious ejection of the invading armies of Napoleon and Hitler. In fact, the British and French allies fought for a limited objective of restraining Russian expansion to the Eastern Mediterranean and did not attempt to conquer the country. Probably the conflict in the Crimea was almost irrelevant to the outcome of the war, which was principally determined by an effective naval blockade of St Petersburg by the British and French navies.

Fighting ceased about sixteen months after the surrender of Sevastopol with the Russian retirement. Allied armies (British, French, Turkish and Sardinian) remained in occupation until the peace treaty was signed in Paris. During the period of truce cemeteries were created. It is not clear whether these were paid for by public funds or by the families of the men killed. The middle of the nineteenth century was the time of the development of what were called Garden Cemeteries all over the world. For hygienic reasons, there was great concern toward the bodies of the dead from congested churches in city centres and a move for burial outside city limits, as had been done in Ancient Greece. The word cemetery was derived from Greek for 'sleeping place'. Major cemeteries were laid out at Père La Chaise in Paris, Kensal Rise in London and in North and South America; Boston and Buenos Aires. The army sought to replicate, so far as possible, the cemeteries that would be constructed at home.

In the years after the war the tombstones of the British dead were moved to Cathcart's Hill, Sevastopol, now Ukraine, although the bodies of the dead were not disturbed. This is in contrast to the practice of the military burial authorities in the British and American armies which sought after the Great War to rebury the bodies of their dead.

Following the war, the combatant powers erected many memorials to their war dead and indeed to their leaders. There are still hundreds, if not thousands, of Russian memorials in the Crimea. Many were damaged in the Second World War in fierce fighting by the German invading army, but have subsequently been restored. Until the Second World War foreign memorials in the Crimea had been reasonably well maintained. Until the Bolshevik

Revolution the British consul in Sevastopol took care of the memorial on Cathcart's Hill, where there was a small museum for which the Consul was also responsible. After the Bolshevik Revolution, the Russian authorities assumed responsibility for the maintenance of the sites and were reimbursed their expenses by the foreign governments.

In the tense period of the Cold War after the Second World War, on Khrushchev's instructions, many of the cemeteries and memorials erected by the allies in the Crimea were destroyed. In the past few years, this damage has for the most part been restored with the French cemeteries largely restored and the British monuments repaired or replaced. A visit to the area can be confusing to the visitor in trying to decide what is original and what has been replaced. The Russian change of heart seems to be partly due to Glasnost and partly to the acceptance of treaty obligations to respect the memorials of foreign military dead. Major works are still taking place in Russia creating cemeteries for the remains of the German soldiers from the Second World War.

The Crimean War was the first war where the British erected memorials to their military dead. Examples include the Memorial obelisk by Baron Marochetti in Istanbul to British Army and Navy dead, the Memorial to Old Boys of Westminster School who lost their lives in Russia in the Crimean War and Indian (Mutiny) wars and the Memorial erected by Russians to the servicemen who died in prison in Lewes in Sussex.

Whilst travelling through Kiev and in the Crimea, I saw photographs being taken of couples on their wedding day beside the local war memorial. The tradition of laying flowers upon Second World War memorials, expressing gratitude for their lives and happiness, still seems to be a custom in Russia, so intertwined are perceived the fate of the dead and the hopes of the living.

In the Spanish Civil War, after the Nazi attack on the Northern Spanish town Guernica, Pablo Picasso (*1881-1973*) produced a great propaganda picture. The Basque town of Guernica was destroyed in a bombing raid as an event to celebrate Hitler's birthday on April 20th, which was planned by Herman Goering, the commander of the German Air Force. The raid was designed to kill as many people as possible. The attack was delayed and did not take place until 26th April, 1937. The following day Radio Bilbao broadcast the news that more than fifteen hundred civilians had been annihilated.

In Paris, Picasso could usually be found at the Café de Flore, and the poet Juan Larrea, the Director of Information at the Spanish Embassy, heard the news and drove to the cafe. Four months earlier the artist had been commissioned to paint a mural for the Spanish Republican Pavilion for the forthcoming 1937 Paris World's Fair. Picasso had been seeking propaganda material and Larrea realised that the obliteration of Guernica would provide Picasso with just the right material for his propaganda. Larrea stated 'it's like a bull in a china shop' when Picasso said he had no idea what a bombed town looked like. Very quickly Picasso began to produce drafts of his proposed painting. This was to be a very large oil on canvas and was completed by June 1937. The picture would emerge as the dominant artistic feature relating to the Spanish Civil War.

The monochrome picture conveys deep emotion through complex symbolism. Picasso said 'It isn't up to the painter to define the symbols. Otherwise, it would be better if he wrote them out in so many words. The public who look at the picture must interpret the symbols as they understand them.' He added that the bull represented brutality and darkness.

After the exhibition closed, the picture was sent on an international tour for nineteen years, raising funds for Spanish refugees. Eventually, Picasso's picture was taken to the United States where it remained until after Franco's death when it was returned to Spain where it can be seen in the Reina Sofia, Spain's National Museum of Art in Madrid. The story of the bombing of Guernica by the Luftwaffe as a birthday present for Adolf Hitler has recently been published.

In Germany, the Nazis removed memorials to the First World War of which they disapproved. The commemoration of the Second World War followed to a great extent the memorialisation of the Great War. Often new lists of names were engraved on existing memorials. Major differences were heavy civilian casualties in air raids, but these millions of deaths did not give rise to many distinguished memorials.

I am surprised that the Germans allowed the memorial by Kathe Kollwitz (1867-1945) in Belgium showing parents mourning the loss of their son to survive the war but perhaps it was overlooked. Kollwitz lost her youngest son, Peter, on the battlefield in Flanders in Belgium 1914. After producing many drafts for a monument to Peter and his fallen comrades she put aside the project in 1919 and began again in 1924. This monument titled *The Grieving Parents*, was finally completed and placed in the war cemetery of Roggevelde in 1932. Later, the statues were moved with Peter's remains when they were relocated to the nearby Vladslo German war cemetery.

When I visited Finland in the late 1990s, I was able to see many memorials. One can trace the movements in Finnish history through its memorials. The somewhat triumphalist memorials erected by the Whites following civil war and the sadder memorials erected by the Reds many years later, make for an interesting comparison. One can see in some of the earlier monuments, the sense of the Finns driving away the Russians.

A sense of the stresses of Finnish history is necessary to appreciate the way memorials have developed. In 1809 Finland ceased to be part of Sweden as the Grand Duchy of Finland became a semi-autonomous part of Russia. In 1917, following the Russian Revolution, Finland, after a civil war, achieved full independence from Russia. The Russian Revolution created a period of great stress in Finland with the collapse of established institutions and a civil war broke out. The anti-communists, the Whites, were fighting for Finnish independence and traditional social values. The Whites, aided by Germany, both on the battlefield and in training troops, overcame the Reds who were seeking to extend the Russian Revolution to Finland. The White forces were led by Marshal Mannerheim (1867-1951), a Finnish officer who had served with distinction in the Tsarist Army for thirty years and who was to dominate Finnish politics for the next quarter of a century.

In Finland, the bodies of soldiers killed in war were returned to their native parishes for burial. Even in the terrible stress of the Winter War, bodies of those killed in action were regularly sent back to their home towns. The military felt that by returning the war dead for burial as heroes in their home parishes, public opinion would be influenced against Russian invaders. Military funerals which were public demonstrations with flags, speeches and flowers, took place and were paid for out of public funds. Families could decide whether their dead should be buried in family graves or in a military section of the local cemeteries. Very few servicemen were buried outside military cemeteries. There are six hundred military graveyards in Finland. Nearly every military cemetery has war memorials financed and chosen by local people.

Memorials put up for the Whites immediately after the Civil War seek to show the triumph of civilisation over the forces of the barbarism from the East and the memorial in Helsinki to Finnish soldiers by the sculptor Elias Ilkka (1889-1968), and the architect Erik Bryggman (1891-1955) is in this style. Bas-reliefs on a black granite memorial depict youths on horseback with a youth holding the harness of a horse.

The Civil War memorial in Tampere sculpted by Viktor Jansson (1896-1958), is a naked man with a sword held aloft, displaying calm in the moment of victory. This classical style is similar to that of the black granite sarcophagus memorial to German soldiers who fell in the Battle for Helsinki in April 1918.

A memorial to the Reds who were executed or died in prison camps, was erected in 1949. The design was by Uuno Inkinen (1913–) who won a competition organised by the Workers Art

Club. The year 1918 has been cut in the front of the stone with a soldier lying on the ground. Beside the soldier is a child with arms extended, with her grieving mother. The text carved on the memorial refers to those who fought in the class war and became victims of the revenge of the whites. This memorial is on a military base and is difficult to visit. The Reds, unlike the Whites, did not receive honoured burial. Many women fought for the Reds and were killed or executed by the Whites. Finland was a pioneer in the emancipation of women and was one of the first countries to give women the vote.

*Monument to the Reds at Lahti*

The oversize monument to the Reds at Lahti in Fellman Park designed by Erkki Kannosto (*1945–*) was built on the sixtieth anniversary of the ending of the Finnish Civil War. Dedicated to all the red prisoners it is situated on the site of the largest red prisoner camp of 1918, and features five huge bronze figures.

For a country with a population of five million, Finland has a remarkable collection of memorials of exceptional quality to those killed in war. This reflects the absolute determination of a small country to maintain its independence in the face of what, on any normal military analysis, would appear to be overwhelming odds in the conflicts of the twentieth century.

# ✧ Chapter Six ✧
# The Home Front

*The Afgan Memorial Church*

$S$ince retirement, my study of war memorials has increased, particularly ones nearer my home. I have given lectures on local memorials which led to a greater interest in the artists and sculptors, in particular Edward Lutyens, in my opinion, the greatest British architect of the twentieth century. Our house here in Sussex, was designed by a Lutyens enthusiast and reflects our taste. He was a clean and clear architect with some excellent use of colours and was also an exceptionally interesting person famous for his wit.

A mural in our dining room was painted by the well-known professional artist Elizabeth Butler from Amberley, West Sussex and depicts a number of monuments in a unique setting. On the left of the picture, you will see a monument from Boston, Massachusetts of Colonel Shaw and his African American infantry from the American Civil War. Then, tucked on the side of a hill, is part of the Cenotaph in Whitehall in London, by Lutyens. A little further over you will see a monument to the Missing on the Somme, also by Lutyens. The setting is vaguely supposed to be the Arun Valley, but I think the colours are what I associate with summer in Southern Iran.

Tucked away among the trees you will see our house and beside it Wiggonholt Church. Past that high on the side of the Downs you see the Chattri and then as you move along you will see another Lutyens monument, The India Gate in New Delhi

Lutyens spent many years working for the British Government in India on the construction of New Delhi and was sensitive to Indian opinion – he opposed Christian symbolism which he felt would be unpopular in India. India was then the most important part of the British Empire.

Lutyens worked with the Imperial War Graves Commission and designed The All-India War Memorial Arch, more popularly known as The India Gate, in New Delhi in memory of the fallen soldiers of the First World War and Afghan Wars. This was one of over sixty memorials he designed in Europe.

Lutyens was a major artist of the time responsible for the elegant memorial to Raymond Asquith (*1878-1916*), son of Herbert Asquith the prime minister, in Amiens Cathedral in France. Raymond Asquith's death in action on the Somme on 15th September 1916 was a national shock. My mother, who was then a little girl, said it was the first event outside the family she remembered. Winston Churchill wrote of Asquith: 'The war which found the measure of so many never got to the bottom of him, and when the Grenadiers strode into the crash and thunder of the Somme, he went to his fate cool, poised, resolute, matter of fact and debonair.'[5] Raymond's death was a profound blow to his father who lost the will to continue in office and after a few months was supplanted as prime minister by David Lloyd George.

Raymond Asquith's grave may be seen in the Guillemont Road Cemetery, Guillemont and his name features on a number of war memorials. Raymond's name is also on the memorial at Mells with that of his brother-in-law Edward Horner and the other men from the village who lost their lives.

Edwin Lutyens visited Mells to design the

village war memorial and wrote to his wife, 'My weekend was a spring day, fun and tears. All their young men are killed'. In the village church is a memorial tablet to Raymond, designed by Lutyens and with lettering by Eric Gill. The church also contains an equestrian statue by Sir Alfred Munnings of Edward Horner, killed at the battle of Cambrai in 1917. Horner seems rather wooden but the horse is excellent.

*Memorial to Edward Horner, Mells*

\* \* \*

The Afghan Memorial Church in Bombay, (now Mumbai) was the first neo-gothic church in India and was erected to the memory of the British and Indian soldiers who lost their lives in the First Afghan War – the greatest disaster in British military history until the fall of Singapore in 1941.

In 1839, the British, nervous of Russian influence in Central Asia, attempted to take control of Afghanistan, sending an army of four thousand men to Kabul and placing a British nominee on the throne. In the face of a popular uprising, the British garrison was attacked by local people and nearly everyone was killed. The British agreed to leave under the promise of safe conduct but the British Army was attacked on its withdrawal to India – the Afghans breaking the agreement as they were keen to get rid of the British for good. The Afghans perhaps felt they had a wonderful opportunity to take the British Army by surprise. Every man except one, a doctor who escaped, was killed or taken prisoner.

The Afghan Memorial Church was designed using the principles of gothic architecture advanced by Augustus Pugin (1812-1852). Plans for the quintessentially

English neo-Gothic architecture of the church were submitted in 1847 by the city engineer of Bombay Henry Conybeare (*1823-1892*) and approved. Early English in style with a tall tower and a spire of one hundred and eighty-nine feet (fifty-eight metres), the church is an unmissable landmark, visible from a distance even from the sea. It was traditionally the first sight of India by arriving British troops. Fine stained glass in the narrow lancet windows show regiments of the British or the East India Company's Army. The East India Company was formed as a trading company and it had a separate military and political establishment to the British Government in India. The East India Company employed British soldiers with many Indians soldiers to defend its properties and maintain its power.

In the church, the chancel is paved with English encaustic tiles (ceramic tiles with two or more different coloured clays inlaid and fired to make a decorative pattern). The ornamental illuminated screen is a later addition by William Butterfield (*1814-1900*). Many of the fittings were made by the Bombay School of Art where Rudyard Kipling's father, Lockwood Kipling (*1837-1911*), was principal from 1865-1875.

I have no doubt the power and importance of the memorial is both the beauty of the architecture and the tragedy of the loss of the men of the British expeditionary force in Afghanistan.

The Chattri is a remarkable memorial which commemorates Indian soldiers who died on active service in Europe with the British Army during the war of 1914-18, and whose bodies were cremated on the South Downs close to Brighton. The Indians, mostly peasant folk, reinforced the British Army as it struggled to block the Germans from the Channel Ports. They fought in the freezing dirt of Flanders against Germany's fearsome, well-trained and fully-equipped troops, and few survived. Above all it is a distinguished and beautiful work of art in the Sussex countryside, a reminder of the splendour of British India, memories that Indians living in this country share with the local population.

'Chattri' is an Urdu word meaning shelter or umbrella. The memorial is an octagonal dome made of white Sicilian marble, supported by eight pillars and is twenty-nine feet high on a stone plinth. Three granite rocks cover the concrete cremation pit in which the bodies were burnt in accordance with Hindu and Sikh funeral customs. Guidance on the form of the Chattri came from Sir Swinton Jacob (*1841-1917*), a distinguished architect whose career had started as an engineer in the Indian Army and who subsequently practised for many years as an architect in India. Detailed drawings were produced by E C Henriques, a student in England from Mumbai (Bombay),

*The Chattri, Brighton*

who later returned to India where he had a distinguished career, and became President of the Indian Institute of Architecture during the Second World War.

The Chattri, listed as Grade II was erected in 1921 and unveiled by the Prince of Wales, later King Edward VIII. A new screen wall listing the names and regiments of the men whose bodies were cremated on the site, was unveiled by the Commonwealth War Graves Commission in September 2010. The number of deaths with fifty-three cremations was comparatively small compared with the heavy casualties suffered in the field, but few of the wounded survived to travel from France and most of the patients in Brighton were convalescents.

An inscription in English, Hindi and Urdu reads:

*'To the memory of all Indian soldiers who gave their lives for the King Emperor in the Great War. This monument erected on the funeral pyre, where Hindus and Sikhs who died in hospital at Brighton passed through the fire, is in grateful admiration and brotherly affection dedicated.'*

The wording was devised by Sir John Otter, the mayor of Brighton during the war, who organised the appeal and funds and the construction of the memorial. He suggested two memorials, one on the cremation site on the Downs and one at the Royal Pavilion, which was used as a hospital during the war. The India Office (the government department then responsible for British rule in India) agreed to pay half the cost of the memorial on the Downs with the corporation paying the other half and accepting responsibility for future maintenance.

In the early part of the war, Indian soldiers serving in France who were wounded or sick were brought to England for treatment. Military hospitals for these soldiers were established in Sussex and Hampshire. Brighton Corporation, which owned the Royal Pavilion, made it available for the use of the army. John Nash's oriental design looks Indian and out of place in Brighton but somewhat quixotically it was felt that Indian soldiers, who mostly lived in villages or barracks, would feel more at home in the oriental splendour of this former British royal palace. Other buildings, including the workhouse in Brighton, were used as hospitals for the Indian military.

Great care was taken in adapting the Royal Pavilion to the dietary and caste requirements of the patients. They were catered for by nine kitchens and two distinct supplies of water, one for Hindus and one for Muslims. The army authorities wished the Indian patients to be as well treated as wounded British soldiers. King George V and Queen Mary, accompanied by Lord Kitchener, visited the hospital on several occasions. A film was also made of the treatment of Indian patients in the hospital and shown to soldiers at the Front.

In thanks to the people of Brighton who cared so well for their men, the people of India gave a North Indian-style Memorial Gate to the Pavilion, designed and made in Britain by Thomas Tyrwhitt. Known as the Indian Gate, it was unveiled in 1921 by the Maharaja of Patiala.

In the years after the war until the 1940s, the Chattri was neglected, but with the increasing Indian population in Britain, it has become a place of pilgrimage. Each year, there is a service of commemoration on the last Sunday in June attended by many Indians and members of the local community. Organisations in the hands of the local Sikh, the High Commissioner of India and his military attaché attend remembrance ceremonies there and many members of the local Indian population now attend.

Controversially by today's standards, the local authorities were worried about the risks of introducing large numbers of men from India to British society in case they became involved with local women. The Viceroy himself wrote from India saying that European nurses should not look after Indian patients.

At a different level, there was anxiety about the presence of thousands of trained armed Indian troops in Britain. The Indian Mutiny of 1857 was just within living memory. John Buchan's novel Greenmantle, about a German plan to raise the Muslims of the East against the British Empire, was not wholly fanciful. Indeed, Buchan has said that the alleged disloyalty of the Indian Army was a major factor in German war calculations. His fears were unfounded, though the British government did establish a team of civil servants and officers from India, fluent in local languages, to censor the mail of Indian soldiers, looking for evidence of instability or disloyalty among those serving in Europe.

Rudyard Kipling (1865-1936) who lived at Burwash, close to Brighton, visited the patients in hospital in 1915. Kipling wrote four short stories called 'The Eyes of Asia', as though from Indian patients in Britain to their families in India. Kipling had not lived in India for many years before he wrote the book, and took careful advice not to make errors of Indian customs or caste. These stories followed a request in 1916 for Kipling to cooperate with the British authorities in producing propaganda to assist the war effort. Kipling was supplied, in great secrecy, translations of letters sent home by Indian soldiers in hospital in Britain, which formed the basis of his semi-fictional accounts. 'The Eyes of Asia' is still in print.

Kipling's ambition was that his son John should have a career in the armed services, whose members he so much admired. Kipling's companions at school were mostly the sons of serving officers and his attitude was greatly influenced by experiences in India and in South Africa. John inherited his father's poor eyesight which ruled out a naval career. John was sent to Wellington, a public school with a strong army tradition. John's eyesight continued to deteriorate and when he tried to join up in 1914 he failed two army medical boards. Only after an intervention by Field-Marshal Lord Roberts, an old friend of his father's, did John secure a commission in the Irish Guards, apparently without a medical – probably a danger to himself and to the men he commanded.

Kipling's wife, Carrie (*1863-1939*), in a letter to her mother written in October 1914, said:

*'One mustn't let one's friends' and neighbours' sons be killed in order to save us and our son. There is no chance John will survive unless he is so maimed from a wound as to be unfit to fight. We know it and he does. We all know it, but we all must give and do what we can and live on the shadow of a hope that our boy will be the one to escape.'* [6]

When the news came that John was missing, the Kiplings in public maintained a brave face, optimistic that he would be found, but in private the position was different. Julia Depew, an American friend, saw them in their London hotel in December 1915, but as she left, Rudyard said, out of Carrie's earshot: *'Down on your knees, Julia, and thank God you do not have a son.'*

Following the loss of his son John who had been reported missing at the Battle of Loos in September 1915, Rudyard Kipling's work in the commemoration of the dead of the Great War took other forms. Enquiries about John Kipling's fate in battle and the erection of memorials to his memory were an important part of Kipling's life for many years.

During the war, Kipling's health deteriorated with constant stomach pains, which seem to have begun with John's army service and the anticipation of his death. Kipling had to absorb the shock of the disappearance of John's generation of young men and tried to come to terms with a situation in which many families suffered bereavement from the war.

Kipling's health did not stabilise for nearly twenty years until a duodenal ulcer was diagnosed and treated. Meanwhile he was in constant pain and consulted many doctors without help.

In 1917, Kipling became a member of the Imperial War Graves Commission, which had been established to register, mark and tend the graves of British soldiers. Planning started while the war was in progress, and the Commission sent Edwin Lutyens and Herbert Baker, the two leading architects of their generation, to France to advise on the design and layout of the cemeteries.

Until the First World War, arrangements for the burial of British soldiers killed in war had been haphazard and irregular. At the beginning of the war, there was no official organisation responsible for the burial of men killed in action. At first this duty was handled by a Red Cross organisation headed by Fabian Ware, a former journalist without military experience. As the scale of the casualties became apparent, the army provided personnel for the recording and burial of the dead. Bodies were buried where possible, in individual graves marked with temporary wooden crosses. Ware, with the rank of Major General, became head of the Army Graves Service.

Kipling's main contribution was the drafting of inscriptions used by the Commission. On the graves of those for whom a name could not be found, he produced 'A soldier of the Great War known unto God'. On the Great Stone of Remembrance placed at military cemeteries, he chose the phrase from Ecclesiastes 'their name liveth for ever more'. For those whose burial places had been destroyed by shelling, he wrote 'Their glory shall not be blotted out'.

Kipling did not want to use the language of Christianity because he felt this might be offensive to Hindus and Muslims who served in the Indian Army, and perhaps this would also conflict with his own position as a non-believer. Kipling's phrase 'Lest we Forget', used in a different context in his poem Recessional, was often used on war memorials, particularly in the United States, but less commonly in Britain.

For some time, the King and others had been trying to persuade Kipling to accept the Order of Merit. In the summer of 1921 Lord Stamfordham wrote on behalf of the King offering the OM and Kipling replied on 17th December declining the honour.

In January 1922 Kipling was approached by several newspapers asking to confirm or deny whether he had been offered the OM. Carrie Kipling wrote in her diary, *'Rud upset by wires from newspapers about the report of OM.'* [7] On 16th January Lord Stamfordham wrote to Kipling taking responsibility for the newspaper reports.

The King's Pilgrimage story is not set out in any of the biographies of Kipling which I have read and what is not included is Kipling's meeting with Lord Stamfordham on 2nd February. The following is based on information I obtained from the Royal Archives at Windsor Castle and is an extract from Lord Stamfordham's note of the meeting, which reads as follows:

*'He (Mr Rudyard Kipling) then proceeded to say how important it was that the King should visit the graveyards in France and Flanders. Mr Kipling is in touch with republican propaganda and knows what capital is made out of this omission*

*in unfortunately criticising the King, especially in Australia and South Africa, but generally throughout the Dominions and Crown Colonies. I mentioned this to the King.'* [8]

This must, one feels, have followed the upset over the leak to the press and it seems that Kipling's idea of a visit by the King to the cemeteries may have been accepted partly as a peace offering. Subsequently Carrie Kipling wrote in her diary, *'Rud ... is glad he proposed it and it was acted on.'* [9]

It is generally accepted that Kipling wrote the great speech made by King George V at the end of his visit to the war cemeteries:

*'Never before in history have a people dedicated and maintained individual memorials to their fallen and in the course of my Pilgrimage I have many times asked myself whether there can be a more total advocate of peace upon earth through the years to come, than this massed multitude of silent witnesses to the desolation of War.'* [10]

Certainly, this is the view of his biographers. Carrie, in her diary, recorded that Rudyard was working on a speech for the King. Fabian Ware in sending the final draft to the Palace said it had been discussed with Kipling. Correspondence between Kipling and Fabian Ware of the Imperial War Graves Commission indicates that the speech that Kipling had prepared was well received at the Palace.

It is a wonderful speech, but the statement that: *'Never before in history have a people dedicated and maintained individual memorials to their fallen'* is quite wrong, as anyone who has been to Arlington, Gettysburg or the other American Civil War cemeteries would have known.

*Kipling and King George V*

One feels that Kipling would not have made such a mistake. Married to an American, he had lived in the United States for four years and was keenly interested in history. When the Kiplings were living in Vermont, Civil War memorials were being erected all over the country. Kipling was familiar with Lincoln's speech at Gettysburg and said Lord

Birkenhead's speech, as Secretary of State for India, at the dedication of the memorial for the Indian Army soldiers at Neuve-Chapelle, was the finest funeral oration since Gettysburg. This praise might have been given for the King's Speech. Kipling visited Washington and it seems unlikely that he did not go to the National Cemetery at Arlington. As an inveterate tourist, it seems curious that Kipling did not visit Gettysburg, which in the 1890s was not a difficult train journey from Washington.

Curiously, the King's speech did not raise comment at the time. Winston Churchill, who was Secretary of State for War, had an American mother, was a keen historian and might have noticed the mistake. Lord Curzon, former Foreign Secretary, had been married to two American women and was involved with the commemoration of the war dead. Curzon devised the Armistice Day ceremonies which are still used every year at the Cenotaph and throughout the Commonwealth. Many soldiers who were present, including Field Marshal Haig, would have studied the American Civil War as part of their military education and yet no one seems to have commented on this error.

The visit to the war cemeteries was followed by a book, *The King's Pilgrimage* not written by Kipling but edited by him. The book sold well but produced a comment from the Palace that perhaps not sufficient prominence had been given to the role of General Haig in the Pilgrimage. Kipling felt that Haig's tactics were one reason for his son's death and shared the general critical view in England of his generalship. Indeed, when asked to compose an epitaph for Haig's grave at Dryburgh Abbey, his non-committal inscription was, 'This cross of sacrifice is identical with those that stand above the dead of Lord Haig's armies in France and Flanders'

The Pilgrimage to the war cemeteries was the beginning of Kipling's friendship with the King and his role as a royal speech writer. Kipling became a regular visitor to Buckingham Palace. Kipling wrote speeches for other members of the royal family and helped his cousin, Stanley Baldwin, with his speeches. According to Stanley's son Oliver, as told to the Kipling Society in 1971, the famous phrase Baldwin used of newspaper proprietors, 'Power without responsibility, the prerogative of the harlot throughout the ages,' came originally from Kipling. [11]

In 1927 Kipling attended the dedication of the memorial designed by Herbert Baker to the soldiers of the Indian Army and their British officers killed in France. Herbert Baker was an architect to the Commission and responsible for some of its most important structures in France, including the Tyne Cot cemetery near Ypres and the Indian Army memorial at Neuve-Chapelle. This design was inspired by Baker's knowledge of Indian architecture and based on his work for the capital of India in New Delhi. Kipling had known Baker since they had been together in South Africa at the time of the Boer War, when Baker built the house provided for the Kipling family by Cecil Rhodes.

Not all war memorials have survived but a surprising number are venerated and well maintained.

The execution of Nurse Edith Cavell (1865-1915) by the German Army in Brussels in 1915 was a cause célèbre in the Great War. Cavell, daughter of a Norfolk vicar, was managing a training school for nurses in Brussels when war broke out in 1914. She remained at her post when many other British nurses returned home. When French and British soldiers made their way to Brussels from the battlefields, it was she who helped them to cross the frontier into neutral Holland, where they were able to rejoin their regiments.

The German military authorities thought correctly that this was a breach of the laws of war and that Red Cross personnel should maintain strict neutrality. The Germans court-martialled Nurse Cavell and she was sentenced to death by firing squad. This sparked a new wave of anti-German publicity on the grounds that this was the kind of frightfulness that had given the occupying forces such a bad reputation in Belgium. Cavell became a great heroine in the English-speaking world because of her exemplary courage.

Substantial funds were raised from the public to pay for a monument of Cavell, designed by Sir George Frampton, one of the leading British sculptors of the period. The statue was erected in 1922, close to the National Portrait Gallery at St Martin-in-the-Fields.

The marble figure of Cavell is some ten feet tall, set against a block of granite which reaches another fifteen feet above her. 'This spread,' wrote General Gleichen in his book on London's Open-Air Statuary, 'though somewhat incomprehensibly, into the form of a cross beautiful half figure of a woman with a child representing humanity protecting the Small State.'

*Memorial to Edith Cavell,*
*St Martin-in-the-Fields, London*

The statue bears the words, 'Humanity, Fortitude, Devotion and Sacrifice'. There is also a plaque that reads:

*'Edith Cavell, Brussels, Dawn October 12th, 1915.*

*'Patriotism is not enough. I must have no hatred or bitterness for anyone.'*

The statue was unveiled in 1920 by Queen Alexandra, widow of King Edward VII. Someone said to Margot Asquith, wife of former prime minister Herbert Asquith, that the Germans will be ashamed when they see the statue. Margot responded, 'not as ashamed as the British will be.' Was she referring to the sheer size of the statue in its diminutive setting? Perhaps the sum of money raised was so large that Frampton felt he had to produce a monument to match.

The Germans felt they were unfairly criticised for the execution of Edith Cavell who, in their view, was a war criminal. The Kaiser was so concerned by the strong reaction from the Allies that he issued orders that no other women should be executed without his consent.

Hitler seems to have shared the indignation of the German Army. When he paid a lightning visit to Paris after the collapse of France in 1940, he ordered that Cavell's monument there should be destroyed. The army also destroyed the Cavell monument in Brussels. While the latter was repaired after the war, the Paris monument was lost to history, and it is difficult to find a photograph that captures its quality.

And so, the London monument to Cavell remains a bastion of perseverance and lasting fortitude. Her courage has made her a heroine all over the English-speaking world. Buildings, many streets in France, wards in hospitals, indeed hospitals themselves have been named after Edith Cavell. A mountain was also named for her in the Canadian Rockies.

Along with Lutyens (1869-1944), C.S. Jagger (1885-1934) was probably the most famous British artist to emerge from the First World War. Jagger is responsible for the Artillery Memorial at Hyde Park Corner in London, and for many other distinguished war memorials.

Jagger wanted to be a sculptor but his father insisted that he should learn a trade. At the age of fourteen he was apprenticed to Mappin & Webb in Sheffield as a metal engraver. Without telling his family, he applied to the Royal College of Art in London in 1907 and won a scholarship. He studied sculpture in the traditional way and he developed his craft by copying from the antique. The metalworking skills he had learnt at Mappin & Webb enabled him to work as easily in metal as stone. Much of Jagger's stonework has been seriously damaged by pollution in the twentieth century. It is difficult now to discern the stone carving on the figures on the artillery memorial and on the navy war memorial at Portsmouth. The least damaged of Jagger's stone carvings are those at Louveral near Cambrai in France, showing men struggling to move a casualty across a trench.

After leaving art school, Jagger supported himself by working as an assistant to his former teacher, Professor Edouard Lantéri and teaching as an instructor in modelling at the Lambeth School of Art. In 1914, he won the Prix de Rome which gave him a three-year scholarship at the British School in Rome. However, war came and Jagger at once joined the Artists Rifles. He served in Gallipoli and in France, was gassed three times, and was twice wounded sufficiently badly to be repatriated to Britain. Jagger was awarded the Military Cross and had, in the language of the period, a 'good war'.

In 1919, the British School in Rome gave Jagger an award to replace his original scholarship. He produced 'No Mans Land' showing a soldier crouching at a listening post on the battle field trying to hear what was happening in the German trenches. The listener is surrounded by the bodies of dead soldiers, some hanging as though crucified on the wire. The first version of the work had carved upon it a verse:

*'O little mighty band that stood for England*
*That with your bodies a living shield*
*Guarded her slow awakening'*
Beatrix Brice-Miller (1877-1959)

These lines are not on the bronze cast given to the Tate Gallery by the British School in Rome in 1923. Currently displayed at Tate Britain, the piece was withdrawn from public exhibition in 1938 and was not shown again for many years.

Jagger produced a series of war memorials with strong figures. For example, the war memorial at Grange Hill, Hoylake and West Kirby, on one side of the monument, a soldier is standing holding his rifle firmly on guard and on the other there is a figure of a woman in mourning. Mourning women are rare on war memorials in Britain although not uncommon in France. Jagger's service background enabled him to put forward ideas which might have been resisted from a more conventional artist. Also like Lutyens, Jagger had the skill of a charming personality and persuading his clients to accept advice which they might have otherwise found unacceptable. However, Jagger's approach to war commemoration meant that he was unable to find a commission for one of his most poignant memorials. This shows a soldier standing mourning at the grave of a friend. This monument was not erected but there are maquettes at the Historial de la Grande Guerre at Peronne and at the Sheffield City Art Gallery.

The Royal Artillery War Memorial Committee wished to have a monument incorporating a gun. The leading artists of the period, Edwin Lutyens, Herbert Baker and Dermot Wood all resisted this approach. However, John Singer Sargent, the famous American portrait painter, recommended Jagger who appreciated military sensibilities. Jagger was given the commission and allowed to nominate as his architect Lionel Pearson. Pearson was also responsible for the Sandham Memorial Chapel, with Stanley Spencer's war murals. Jagger worked well with the Royal Artillery and persuaded the committee to allow him to introduce as a late change, the body of a soldier lying under his greatcoat.

Time has led to a general acceptance of the special quality of the figures of the men of the Artillery Memorial, Hyde Park Corner, London. The captain, the driver and the shell carrier, standing round the stone base of a great artillery field piece, with the body of a soldier covered by his great coat lying at the rear. Bodies of the dead are rarely seen in British memorials. There is carving in the stone on the base of the gun showing equipment being hauled up by the horse artillery with other carvings depicting signallers and telephonists at work in the field.

*Artillery Memorial, Hyde Park Corner, London*

At first the monument was fiercely attacked. Lord Curzon (who knew a great deal about architecture) said it resembled a 'toad squatting, which is about to spit fire out of its mouth – nothing more hideous could ever be conceived'.

*Artillery Memorial, Hyde Park Corner, London*

One reaction is that the massive stone gun does not create the setting Jagger's work deserves, but perhaps a stronger architect such as Lutyens, would not have designed a monument which would have been primarily a vehicle for Jagger's' work. (One reason for the criticism of the monuments put up to the Boer War period, which were primarily sculpture, may have been the desire of architects to secure more of the memorial work after the First World War).

While Jagger was working on the artillery memorial, King George V and his sister used to pass regularly riding from Buckingham Palace to Rotten Row (imagine what a journey this would be in modern traffic). The King used to pause in his ride and ask Jagger how the work was proceeding. Apparently, King George V was a considerable gossip and such an act would not be out of character. I was told about it long ago by C.S. Jagger's daughter, Gillian Jagger, who repeated the story recently.

Jagger became a close friend of Lutyens who was godfather to one of his children. Lutyens asked Jagger to produce miniature bronze busts of Admiral Beatty and Field Marshall Haig for Queen Mary's dolls' house completed in 1924 and found in the Royal Collection in Windsor Castle.

As war memorials work declined in the 1930s, Jagger began to work closely with Lutyens on the construction of New Delhi. This was a modern city erected by the British for a capital in India. Lutyens asked Jagger to help with the ornamentation of his great new city. Jagger was sensitive to Indian aspirations and supplied models for statues which were executed by Indian craftsmen. Jagger's most enduring work were the carved elephants outside the President's house, Raj Bhavan formerly the Viceroy's House.

*Raj Bhavan's House*

Jagger also provided carving for the Jaipur Column in the courtyard approaching Raj Bhavan. Part of the carving on the Jaipur Column was removed as being politically incorrect in post-independent India in the 1950s. Jagger may have designed the line of lions which stood guarding the approach to the official residence. When I visited Raj

Bhavan a major political crisis was taking place and the courtyard area full of television crews. I could not see the statues nor are they apparent in the photographs in the *Millennium Book of New Delhi* (OUP, New Delhi, 2001). I am wondering if Jagger in fact designed these lions and whether they are still in place.

Jagger also started work on a statue of King George V originally sited on Rajpath and now standing on a dilapidated spot at Coronation Park in North Delhi where it is used as a wicket of a cricket pitch by local boys quoted as Britain's greatest legacy to India. Jagger's health was failing and the statue was completed by Sir William Reed Dick. Jagger died suddenly in 1934.

Some years ago, when I was visiting New Delhi with members of the Indian National Trust looking at the site of King George V statue I said, 'If you don't want him please could we have our old King back?' This idea was rejected and I was told this had been proposed by Prince Charles who had been turned down. In fact, the statue is so large it would be very difficult to find a site anywhere in London even in the Royal Parks. Perhaps it would have to go to Windsor Great Park.

# ✧ Chapter Seven ✧
# Death and Glory

HMS Indefatigable
✝
1017

*The Battle of Jutland Memorial*

My father used to say that war was the principal recreation of the human race. I never knew whether he made this up for himself or he found it somewhere in a book. Captain Cook, the explorer and cartographer, wrote about the inhabitants of New Zealand 'for it appears from their numbers of weapons and dexterity in using them, that war is their principal profession'. I think there is considerable truth in such a saying. On the other hand, I get the impression that people who read about war have a rather schoolboy approach to the activity and do not want to be reminded that many deaths in great pain are the inevitable consequence.

I have given talks on the subject of war memorials in the hope of meeting others interested in memorials of this kind and to stimulate discussion of the horrors of wars to try to make future wars less likely. I talked to the War Memorials Trust and the National Army Museum and spoken at a conference in Dublin about memorialisation of the war dead in Ireland.

I detect a rising tide of interest in the subject of memorials to the war dead.

A group of neighbours asked me to tea and grilled me hard about my ideas on war memorials and showed interest and curiosity. On another occasion, the man who came to drain our septic tank came into my room for a signature on his chit. He saw my books and files and asked about my interest. He told me he had recently retired and had spent a week cycling round Normandy visiting British, American and German cemeteries for those who died in the landings in 1944.

When I started to become interested in war memorials, I was worried they would disappear and we would lose works of artistic distinction. However, they are mostly well maintained all over the world and new ones are being erected. In March 2017, the Queen unveiled the Iraq and Afghanistan Memorial in Victoria Embankment Gardens, London. The sculpture, a double-sided bronze medallion, hanging between two large monoliths representing Iraq and Afghanistan by Paul Day, is in recognition of military and civilian personnel who were deployed in those countries between 1990 and 2015.

*Iraq and Afghanistan Memorial*

The British government also recently announced the construction of a memorial to British and Commonwealth troops killed in the invasion of Europe in 1944 to be partly funded by a twenty-million-pound government grant. The D-Day memorial to remember the fallen will be unveiled in the French region of Normandy on the seventy-fifth anniversary in 2019. The monument will have the names of the thousands of members of the British armed forces and Merchant Navy who died, as well as those from other nations.

The Danes seem to have come up with a novel approach for a new war memorial. Denmark is constructing a memorial to the men on the ships from both sides who were lost in the Battle of Jutland in 1916. There will be a speaker system so that visitors can hear the accounts of the battle from the point of view of those who took part. Presumably a text will be available in Danish, English and German. This seems to be pioneering in the technology of commemoration to the war dead. The Danes are giving equal prominence to the men of the ships from both sides. So far as I can see, the project has attracted little publicity in this country. One hopes that this may be something which will be of interest. I am wondering whether I should go over to Denmark to have a look but I suspect there is a great deal more construction work to be done before there is much to see. I think it is unique in the history of war for a neutral power to erect memorials to the dead of combatant powers.

As far as the Royal Navy was concerned they appear to have had an advantage. They could read the German naval signals but the Germans could not read the British signals. The Russians found the German code books early in the war and passed them onto the British, not unlike the way the Poles helped the British in their acquisition of German codes in the Second World War.

Apparently after the battle, the Kaiser Wilhelm II gave congratulatory kisses to the German admirals. One thinks this was not a practice followed by King George V and the Royal Navy.

Recently websites have become a means of commemoration for relatives of those who lost their lives in war. Some are semi-official and include newspaper obituaries for the fallen. The freedom of the internet enables families to post memorials to the dead including anti-war propaganda which would not be tolerated in most public places. The war memorial is evolving with modern technology to provide a fascinating reflection of a world involved in continual conflict.

I am fascinated by memorials. War memorials are not only reminders of courage, sacrifice and loss but particularly after the Great

War, represented an outpouring of emotion and regret at our losses in an art form outside the mainstream of artistic taste of the period. Memorials are sadly unsuccessful warnings of the horrors of war.

I believe the aesthetic quality of war memorials has yet to be given the recognition they deserve. I originally set out to write a book solely about war memorials and for some time now, my ambition was, and still is, to produce a book on the worlds one hundred best war memorials. However, as I remembered my experiences when seeing them, I began to realise how much of my life had been shaped by war. This book then developed into part memoir and part celebration of memorials in all their artistic forms. Not glorifying war but commemorating those who died in war.

# ✧ Acknowledgements ✧

Thanks to go to my family Janet, Rose, Florence and Beatrice, who have taken endless trips to look at, inspect and photograph memorials.

Mervyn Matthews, my travelling companion from long ago for his insight over the years.

Jenny Fly who has been our book keeper for nearly twenty years.

Christine Selby, our hard-working secretary who keeps us organised.

Karen Rycroft, my war memorial assistant and researcher for her collaboration.

Isaac Sonsino, for his help and photographs in the USA.

Hugh Gilbert for the photograph of the dining room mural.

Jon Appleton, my encouraging editor.

Marcus Finch, artist for his illustrations.
http://www.marcusfinch.co.uk

I would like to extend my thanks for their speed and efficiency to the members of staff of
The London Library

Many thanks to those people not mentioned who have helped me with my research over the years.

# ✧ Notes ✧

(1)     Roosevelt letter to King George V –
copyright from The Royal Archives

(2)     Rudyard Kipling 'Irish Guards of the
Great War'. Macmillan 1923

(3)     Rudyard & Carrie Kipling's telegram to
Lady Edward Cecil. Copyright The National Trust

(4)     Kipling speech to Winchester College.
The Wykehamist No 548 Dec 1915.

(5)     Winston Churchill quote about
Raymond Asquith. Permission granted from
'churchillpermissions@curtisbrown.co.uk'

(6)     Carrie Kipling letter to her mother 1914.
Taken from Sussex University papers.

(7)     Quote from Carrie Kipling diary 1922.
Copyright from National Trust

(8)     Quote from Lord Stamfordham.
Copyright from the Royal Archives

(9)     Quote from Carrie Kipling diary 1922.
Copyright from National Trust

(10)     Quote from King George V, Flanders.
Copyright from the Royal Archives

(11)     Quote from Rudyard Kipling. Copyright
from National Trust.

# ✧ Sources ✧

*On War* by Carl von Clausewitz
(Random House 1943)

*The Lion's Pride* by Edward Renehan Jr.
(OUP 1998)

Paul Cret newspaper article 1919

Lincoln dedication speech at Gettysburg 1963.
(Declaration of Independence was published
without copyright protection.)

'Victory or Death' letter by Colonel Travis from
the Alamo. Permanently housed in the Texas
State Archives and Library Building in Austin,
Texas.

www.nps.gov

*Curzon* by David Gilmour (Published by John
Murray 2003)

*A Different Guernica* by John Richardson
(Picasso's biographer) *New York Review of Books.*
May 2016

*Great Contemporaries* Churchill. Winston S.
(Thornton Butterworth 1937)

*The Eyes of Asia* by Rudyard Kipling (Doubleday,
Page & Company)

*Lutyens and the Edwardians* by Jane Brown.
(Viking 1996) Edwin Lutyens letter to Emily
Lutyens. 4 August 1919

*My Boy Jack?* by Tonie & Valmei Holt
(Leo Cooper 1998).

National Trust – Rudyard and Carrie Kipling
letters and diaries

*London's Open-Air Statuary* by General
Gleichen 1928 (Longmans Green & Co 1928)

Quote from Stanley Baldwin taken from a
public speech 17th March 1931.

*The Voyages of Captain Cook Volume 2* by
Captain Cook. (London, W. Smith 1842)

# ✧ Index ✧